Praise for *Taking a Long Look*

"Vivian Gornick is more than a formidable intelligence, she's an entire sensibility. The essays collected here show how a mind shapes and becomes itself in engagement with the writers, thinkers, social facts and theories of her many days. The voice, at once her own and the expression of an entire culture—New York, working class, feminist, Jewish, both open-minded and skeptical—is a gift to be handed down from one generation to the next."

Marco Roth, author of *The Scientists*

"We all talk the talk about public intellectuals nowadays. Vivian Gornick walks the walk. The essays in *Taking a Long Look* could not be more direct, more authoritative, more alive with the pleasures of discovery or alert to the ambiguities of argument. Whether writing literary or political criticism, memoir, or feminist polemic, her mastery is assured."

George Scialabba, author of *How to Be Depressed*

"Illuminating and a welcome addition to the astute critic's oeuvre."

Publishers Weekly

"The lasting value of her work lies in her commitment to the question of what it means to feel 'expressive': to experience the feeling that tells a person 'not approximately, but precisely' who they are."

Dayna Tortorici, *New York Review of Books*

"Gornick is one of the most important essayists of all time. Whether writing on the self, feminism, isolation or politics, she is urgent, sharp-eyed and vital. A superb collection."

Sinéad Gleeson, author of *Constellations*

"Gornick's brilliant half-century writing career can't be captured in a single essay or volume. To engage with her writing is to be left wanting more of her writing."

Liza Featherstone, *Jacobin*

"Reading Vivian Gornick often feels like watching someone paint: you're not sure, at first, what it's going to be, but you're happy to follow her brushstrokes as the picture emerges . . . Gornick repeatedly goes further, looks longer, risks more."

Claire Lowdon, *Times Literary Supplement*

"An engaging collection of sharp, lively essays."

Kirkus Reviews

"*Taking a Long Look* is a magisterial volume of essays which span fifty years of cultural and feminist interrogation."

Lauren LeBlanc, *Observer*

T0286454

Vivian Gornick is a writer and critic whose work has received the Wyndham Campbell Prize, two National Book Critics Circle Award nominations, and been collected in *The Best American Essays 2014*. Her books include the three memoirs *Fierce Attachments*—ranked the best memoir of the last fifty years by the *New York Times*—*The Odd Woman and the City*, and *Unfinished Business: Notes of a Chronic Re-Reader*; as well as *The Romance of American Communism* and the classic text on writing *The Situation and the Story*.

TAKING A LONG LOOK

Essays on Culture, Literature, and Feminism in Our Time

Vivian Gornick

VERSO

London • New York

This paperback edition published by Verso 2022
First published by Verso 2021
© Vivian Gornick 2021, 2022
The publisher and author express their gratitude to the publications
in which earlier versions of these essays appeared. Complete details
of prior publication can be found in the acknowledgments.

1 3 5 7 9 10 8 6 4 2

Verso
UK: 6 Meard Street, London W1F 0EG
US: 388 Atlantic Avenue, Brooklyn, NY 11217
versobooks.com

Verso is the imprint of New Left Books

ISBN-13: 978-1-83976-509-4
ISBN-13: 978-1-78873-979-5 (US EBK)
ISBN-13: 978-1-78873-978-8 (UK EBK)

British Library Cataloguing in Publication Data
A catalogue record for this book is available from the British Library

The Library of Congress Has Cataloged the Hardback Edition as Follows:

Names: Gornick, Vivian, author.
Title: Taking a long look : essays on culture, literature, and feminism in
   our time / Vivian Gornick.
Description: London ; New York : Verso, 2021. | Summary: "For nearly fifty
   years, Vivian Gornick's essays have explored feminism and writing,
   literature and culture, politics and personal experience. Drawing on
   writing from the course of her career, this book illuminates one of the
   driving themes behind Gornick's work: the painful process of
   understanding one's self that binds us to the larger world"— Provided
   by publisher.
Identifiers: LCCN 2020044297 (print) | LCCN 2020044298 (ebook) | ISBN
   9781788739771 (hardback) | ISBN 9781788739795 (ebk)
Subjects: LCGFT: Essays.
Classification: LCC PS3557.O765 T35 2021 (print) | LCC PS3557.O765
   (ebook) | DDC 814/.54—dc23
LC record available at https://lccn.loc.gov/2020044297
LC ebook record available at https://lccn.loc.gov/2020044298

Typeset in Garamond by Biblichor Ltd, Edinburgh
Printed and bound by CPI Group (UK) Ltd, Croydon CR0 4YY

Table of Contents

Introduction

I can remember the exact moment when I left polemical journalism behind me to begin the kind of nonfiction storytelling I had longed, since childhood, to write. One summer morning, on vacation from my job at the crusading *Village Voice* where I wrote most often on behalf of radical feminism, I sat down at a makeshift desk in a beach-front hotel room and found myself typing: "I'm eight years old. My mother and I come out of our apartment onto the second-floor landing. Mrs. Drucker is standing in the open doorway of the apartment next door, smoking a cigarette." These were the first sentences of my memoir, *Fierce Attachments*, and with them I began the long apprenticeship of a writer who, in the act of making naked use of her own undisguised experience, has taught herself to value writing that serves the story rather than writing that imposes itself on the story. By which I mean: as a polemicist I went in search of stories that would illustrate my argument and then used the language I thought would best make it; as a memoirist I developed a set of interacting characters and let them find the language that would best express their situation.

I was in grade school when a teacher held a composition of mine up to the class and said, "This little girl is going to be a writer." I remember being thrilled but not surprised; somehow, the prediction sounded right even then. Decades later, in college, I took the few available writing courses (there were no writing programs then) and again, the teacher (a tough-talking, working-class novelist) pronounced me a writer. This time I was proud because everyone in those classes considered this teacher's nod of approval an anointment. The week before graduation I went up to his desk and stood dumbly before him.

"Yes?" he said.

"What do I do now?" I said.

"Write," he said.

"About what?" I said.

"Kid, get outta here," he said.

So I got myself day jobs—office clerk, per diem high school teacher, editorial assistant—and I wrote. Mainly, I wrote short pieces: my mother and a neighbor talking about an abortion over my four-year-old head, an immigrant marriage in a public garden, a rally at City Hall calling for the mayor's dismissal. Lame, all lame. I'd read these pieces over and I'd see that the language was pedestrian, there was no ruling structure, and the narrative drive was languid.

The problem, I finally understood, was that there was no real point of view; and at last I saw that the point of view was missing because I actually had nothing to say. I was simply accumulating what another writer once called "black marks on a sheet of paper."

Then one evening in the late '60s I was present at a public meeting in which blacks and whites fell out violently over who owned the civil rights movement. The place had exploded with emotion—loud, angry, threatening. I felt the heat building in my chest. I, too, wanted to be heard. But I didn't have the courage to brave the chaos in the room so I determined to commit the scene to paper. I can still feel the urgency I experienced that night as my fingers flew across the keyboard, and the excitement as I worked to disentangle a set of thoughts and emotions that were—transparently!— begging to be made sense of. It came to me that what I wanted badly was to put the reader behind my eyes—see the scene as I had seen it, feel the atmosphere as I had felt it—and to use my own left-leaning, literary-minded self as what I thought of even then as an "instrument of illumination." I had stumbled on the style that was becoming known as personal journalism and had immediately recognized it as my own.

The thing I now find interesting is that in the morning I put the piece in an envelope, took it to the corner mailbox, and without hesitation sent it off to the *Village Voice*. It never occurred to me to send it to the *New Yorker* or the *Times* or any of the many respectable publications then in existence. No, the *Voice*, I instinctively knew, was where I belonged. And, indeed, the *Voice* not only published this piece: within a year I was on its staff where I remained for a good ten years, allowing counterculture journalism to slowly—very slowly—teach me my profession.

It took a while for me to realize that polemics had supplied me with a built-in point of view; and then another, even longer while, to realize that this point of view was articulated by a persona—the narrating voice I pulled from myself to tell the story at hand—that determined everything about the piece: the shape of its structure, the tone of its language, the arc of its direction. Even more important, in time I came to realize that when the sights of this persona were trained outward—that is, on politics and culture—it served one agenda, and when trained inward, another: the first resulted in personal journalism, the second in personal narrative.

But no matter: ultimately everything went back to the dominating question of a point of view. Even though, as I have said, mine at the *Voice* was the inherited one of the born polemicist, just *having* one had taught me to take seriously the matter of knowing when I had something to say, and when I was spinning my wheels and simply putting black marks on a piece of paper. After I'd left the *Voice* and drifted away from openly polemical writing, I saw that, for me, my viewpoint would have to originate elsewhere. I began to write essays, memoirs, book reviews in which I paid more and more attention to a point of view served by an un-surrogated persona who was going to do all in her power to find whatever valuable story was waiting to be rescued from the material at hand.

This book, then, is a collection of pieces written over a period of some forty years that—here organized from the

newest to the oldest—demonstrate, I hope, the apprenticeship of a writer whose critical faculties have been shaped by
the hard-won knowledge that reading into the material is
energizing but reading out of it is infinitely more rewarding.

Vivian Gornick
New York City, 2020

LITERATURE

Lore Segal

In no literature in the world has the immigrant novel been more varied, more original, more persistent than in ours—and this for the most obvious of reasons. The word "America" has been experienced, for at least a hundred and fifty years, by millions all over the world, as a euphemism for the fabled land, where, washing up half drowned on a richly receptive shore, one is assured salvation of an undreamt-of order. So they have been driven to come—wave upon wave upon wave of Jews, Italians, Irish, Latinos, Asians, Africans—and, sooner or later, large numbers of them produce the written document—usually a work of fiction—detailing the disparity between the fantasy and the actuality: the one that is so powerful it seems to the writer that *now* just to utter the word America in quotes is to achieve metaphor.

Only rarely do these novels have a life beyond the one given them on publication day. Even when well written, they are, all too often, claustrophobically enclosed by a tale of survival beyond which America itself remains an abstraction, hardly ever quickening into the life with which a real— rather than a testifying—protagonist would have to engage. A perfect example is Abraham Cahan's 1917 *The Rise of David Levinsky*, an early rags-to-riches story with a strong psychological bent that fails to deepen precisely because Cahan's character is sealed into a ghetto environment that remains static. Levinsky's New York is crowded with Lower East Side Jews who hand him on, one to another, until at last he prospers, but the city itself never emerges as a place of vast and varied doings beyond the streets of the ghetto where the characters soon become indistinguishable. The sole development in the novel, finally, is Levinsky's aware-ness of the absence of development.

Yet the genre is a resilient one. To read an immigrant novel of, say, 1910, one conceived in social realism and sentiment, as contrasted with one written fifty years later, in the wake of Modernism and the Holocaust, is to see how stubbornly it has kept itself alive—and every now and then harbors a piece of work that bursts the bounds of its own conventions, doing everything I just said it rarely does, thereby announc-ing the presence in our midst of a genuine writer.

Lore Segal was born in Vienna in 1928, the daughter of educated, fairly well-to-do Jews. Nine months after Hitler took Austria, she was sent, just ten years old, to England, as part of the rescue mission that came to be known as the *Kindertransport*. The clever little girl wrote an affecting letter to the British refugee committee and within the year her parents, sponsored by well-to-do Brits, were admitted to England as a cook and a butler. For the next seven years the parents worked as a domestic couple in one upper-class house or another, while Lore lived separately, also in one English household after another. When Lore's father died at the end of the war, she and her mother made their way to the Dominican Republic where an uncle was waiting to be admitted to the United States. In 1951 visas came through for the whole family, and Lore's life as a refugee was transformed into that of an immigrant.

Her story took twenty years to tell, and came in two volumes—the first published in 1964 as a fictionalized memoir, *Other People's Houses*, the second in 1985 as the novel *Her First American*. Together, these books reflect, with peculiar power, the change in European literary sensibility brought about by the Second World War, and the one jolted into life by the very American '60s.

Other People's Houses begins in Vienna in the fall of 1937, rapidly sketching in the speed with which the Nazi takeover is accomplished, and the Jews from one day to the next are either running for or losing their lives. In all this mayhem, a little girl of novelistic intelligence and enterprising temperament is caught up, observing herself at the same time that she is being pushed—both frantically and as in a dream—into fear and excitement. When the arrangement is made to secure Lore a place on the first experimental children's transport to England, even as she is feeling "as if my inside had been suddenly scooped away" she thinks, "Wow! I'm off to England!"

This complicated inner circumstance—a sinking heart coupled with unquenchable curiosity—develops in the young Lore what she later called "a survival trick with a price tag." In England, in 1938, the "trick" enabled her to endure brilliantly the double isolation of being separated from her parents, and repeatedly having to absorb the sometimes even greater pain of her refugee status. Early on, she wets her pants and overhears her first foster mother— the self-satisfied Mrs. Levine of Liverpool—say to her daughter, "I told you they don't bring up their children over there as we do here in England." The little girl understands with a shock that she is being perceived as "other."

Watchfulness of a high order becomes second nature to Lore. Called out of class in March of 1939 by the formidable Mrs. Levine to be told that her parents have arrived in England, she listens with the now habituated gravity that Mrs. Levine finds so irritating. "Well! So! Aren't you excited, you funny child!" Yes, Lore tells her, she *is* excited. "But," she tells the reader,

> I was busy noticing the way my chest was emptying, my head clearing, and my shoulders being freed of some huge weight that must, since I now felt it being rolled away, have been there all this time without my knowing it. Just as when the passing of nausea or the unknotting of a cramp leaves the body with a new awareness of itself, sensuously at ease, breathing in and out.

This is the true end of childhood: heedless spontaneity giving way to the self-protection of neutral observation. Standing in a schoolyard among other refugee children, she is told that the parents of a little girl she knows, also in the schoolyard, are dead and that she is now an orphan. Lore stares openly in the child's direction: the word "orphan" interests her. "I kept looking curiously at Helene who was an orphan. She stood by herself in the middle of the schoolyard looking before her. She still wore her little thick coat and her rabbit's-wool hat tied under her chin. One would never have guessed from looking at her that her parents were dead."

It's the tone of the narrating voice in *Other People's Houses* that lends the book its distinction. In other circumstances Lore Segal's predilection for observation without commentary in the face of human extremity might sound slightly mad. But these are *not* other circumstances. These are circumstances that require precisely her degree of remove. An ironic intelligence coupled with a gift for detachment is speaking out of a time and place that strongly encourages what might best be called engaged wariness: precisely the psychological balancing act out of which postwar minimalism was born.

How many European novels of the 1950s have we read in which the reader finds oneself cast adrift on a tide of surreal-sounding prose because while the characters seem ordinary enough, the remove is disorienting: where are we? who is speaking? what are we to make of what is being said? Something stunned, dreamlike, permanently anesthetized in the narration. And then we realize: It's the war that is haunting these pages. The war is the drain, the gap, the terrible lassitude at the heart of the writing.

It is a remarkable memoir indeed that, written in New York City in the late '50s, can so strongly resemble not the structure but the feel of postwar European fiction. While

Other People's Houses is filled with vivid portraits and some marvelous close-ups—England certainly escapes abstraction—what dominates the book is this tone: the tone of one whom history has stunned, and made go cold all over.

Trapped in the Dominican Republic for three years, the full meaning of her permanent statelessness begins to dawn on Lore. Who is she? Where does she belong? What does the future hold? In a paroxysm of youthful defiance (she's now twenty-one years old) she begins to long for England— *that's* who she'll be: English!—carrying around in her head some emblematic memory of geese on a lawn under English trees. But when a woman who works at the British consulate actually provides her with a visa, she freezes.

> I was horrified: Behind the memory of white geese under the great plane trees on the jewel-green lawn appeared, like a double exposure, my bespectacled self, in mackintosh and oxfords, on a cold drizzling English June day, coming across the bridge into Baker Street in such an agony of loneliness that I can recall it in my memory like an event; I remember I stood for a moment to diagnose the cause and felt my feet wet and knew I hadn't a sixpence left for my gas meter.

America, the natural recipient of stateless desolation, it will have to be. It is here and now that the wonderfully chilled Lore of *Other People's Houses* begins the thaw that, twenty-one years later, will release the unmatched vibrancy of *Her First American*.

◡

Twenty-two-year-old Ilka Weissnix, a refugee from Hitler's Europe living in New York's "Washingstein Heights," takes a trip west, gets off the train in Cowtown, Nevada ("I have believed I am being in Utah, isn't it?"), and meets Carter Bayoux (on his way east) in a bar beside the railroad. He is big, he is middle-aged, he is hard-drinking, he is black. Ilka tells Carter that she is looking for the real America, New York is not the real America, there she only meets other refugees. You, she announces triumphantly, are "my first real American." Carter looks at her and replies drily, "Of the second class." What means second class, please? Ilka wants to know. The rest of the book is about how Ilka herself becomes an American as she learns, over the course of a two-year affair with Carter, what means second class please.

Carter Bayoux is one of the great creations in American literature. A black intellectual of the 1950s—journalist, teacher, writer, former advisor to the UN on race relations—he knows "everyone" yet is terminally alone, his spirit howling in the wilderness, doggedly drinking himself to death while begging whatever sympathetic woman comes along to hang in there with him while he destroys himself. Eager, poetic, on-the-brink, sole-survivor Ilka becomes the designated caretaker during one of Carter's last attempts to pull himself out of the void. He, in turn, as they tumble about together, gives her the education of her life, letting her experience New York, the world, and herself—as he does.

In the bar beside the railroad station Carter tells Ilka he's going to teach her how to smoke and drink, and she tells him he doesn't look like a teacher. "What exactly *do* I look like?" he asks. Ilka shakes her head, she cannot find the words in English:

> She meant that she did not recognize his hair, and that the size of his mouth and his laughter did not go with the urbane way he bent his wrist and crossed his ankles; that the luxurious tweed of his jacket contradicted his flattened nose with its small outgrowth of wild flesh at the bridge, which intimated to the girl disastrous chances, moving accidents his youth had suffered.

Later, they take a walk through the garish streets of Cowtown. Passing Harry's Hash and the Steak and Swill, Ilka asks Carter what sort of men these are whom she sees drinking inside. "Good enough fellows," he tells her, "as fellows go—care for their kids, satisfy their wives some of the time, do their work as well as can be expected, and pay their taxes, mostly, go to church, or not, and will string me up as soon as look at me." What means "string you up?" she is thinking, but "I believe *you* have conjured this all, isn't it?" is what she says.

> "I have conjured," said the big American, looking at her. Then he looked deliberately across the street and back at Ilka and said, "You and I stand here, side by side, but I don't know what the hell you're seeing."
> "That *is* it, which I have been meaning," said Ilka with a sensation of bliss. She came, afterward, to identify

this as the moment in which she had fallen in love; it coincided with a break in the traffic and the man's first, slightest touch, under her elbow.

Back in New York, Carter settles into the Bloomsbury Arms (read: Chelsea Hotel) and he and Ilka start the series of mangled dinner dates, disastrous parties, disheveled outings, and emergency rescue calls that becomes their relationship, throughout which Carter sends the bellboy for bourbon, Ilka tries to make him stop drinking, and their conversation mounts in a kind of intelligent hilarity that, for the reader, is pure joy.

Two of the brilliant ingredients Segal throws in to enrich the situation even further is the reappearance of Ilka's mother, a displaced person, whose crazed behavior Carter understands to perfection, and the introduction of a group of Carter's oldest friends, black and white ex-communists who provide Ilka with the excitement of seeing herself in a bad light. Among these people is a couple who seem ill-matched in every way.

"Why would Doris Mae marry . . ." Ilka starts to ask Carter, and stops.

"A Negro twice her age?"

"*You* think I mean *that*"? cried Ilka.

"What *did* you mean?"

"*That!*" said Ilka with a thrill of revelation. "I'm a racist!"

"Not to worry', said Carter. 'Some of my best friends are racists."

This conversation echoes another one in which Carter tells Ilka that when Uptown moves to Washingstein Heights she will move out, everyone does. She thinks this over and insists that she will not.

"You will move," said Carter.
"I will not move," said Ilka.
"You will be the last to move," said Carter, "but you will move."

By the same token, he predicts that sooner or later she will leave him, she will have to. No, Ilka insists, she will not. You will, he mourns. Everyone does. You'll be the last to go, but you will go.

And indeed, within the year she sees what he sees—and feels what he feels:

Carter's door stood ajar. Carter slept with his face to the wall. Ilka made a pass at cleaning up, but there was something ferocious about the mess of soiled clothing, bottles, papers, wires. It came to Ilka—and not for the first time—that she must disengage herself, and the prospect produced a familiar blackness of pain, as if a hand had thrust into her gut and emptied her out.

Exactly what the ten-year-old Lore felt upon being told that she must leave her parents if she was to survive—and exactly what Carter feels all the time.

It was a stroke of genius on Lore Segal's part to see in the character of Carter Bayoux the mirror image that would allow Ilka Weissnix to Americanize her outsiderness. Carter's savvy is so elegant, so original, so bottomless that, exposed to it long enough, Ilka is bound to realize "Oh, *now* I see how it is done."

It is not so much that Carter himself deepens (he simply accumulates); it is his situation that deepens; and as it does, Ilka's clarifies. Carter in America is sufficiently similar to the Jew in Hitler's Europe that she can come to see herself in him. It's this necessary reversal that supplies the book its radiance. The objective correlative to Ilka's growing illumination is the exactly right, real, and convincing way in which her English improves in response to Carter's conversation. As Ilka takes into herself the experience of Carter Bayoux, letting her knowledge of him reshape her, it becomes the key element to how the American language now lives in her. The immigrant experience is completed.

2

Alfred Kazin

The generation of Jewish American writers that was born in the middle of the First World War and came of age in the '30s was destined, in the 1950s and '60s, to revolutionize American literary culture. It was one of those incendiary periods in social history—brought about by the Great Depression and the Second World War—that ended generations of class stability and WASP hegemony. Into this interruption of social certainty poured imaginative writers such as Delmore Schwartz, Saul Bellow, Bernard Malamud, and critical ones such as Leslie Fiedler, Alfred Kazin, Irving Howe, all of whom—having felt stifled by the requirements of high culture—seized the moment to start "speaking" in voices that were so distinctively their own, they could, and often did, seem alarming. An angry fever inhabited the work of many of these writers, one that burned with so singular a strength only the remarkable elasticity of the

American language could take it on. For many of these
writers, the anger never subsided nor did the sense of outsiderness; this, as it turned out, proved both a strength and a
limitation. When the open anti-Semitism which had
dominated these writers' lives subsided, and still they
continued to experience the world as a place of unrelenting
anxiety and frustration, the war against the gentiles was
replaced by one against women. At all times an adversary
was required for the prose to spark itself into life. As they
grew older, many of them discovered that the agent of
aggravation was within. Immutable affliction was the
metaphor that, in their hands, produced literary gold.

Alfred Kazin, one of the stars of this generation of Jewish
American writers, was born in Brooklyn in 1915 into a
family of working-class immigrants. In 1942, at the age of
27, he published a truly seminal book of literary criticism,
On Native Grounds, that made so strong a case for the value
of American literature it helped break the stranglehold that
European fiction had long had on the minds of the
American intelligentsia.

From that moment on, the door to the literary world
began steadily to inch its way open for Kazin, and then
finally it swung wide, whereupon a life of ever-growing
eminence ensued. For more than half a century Kazin
wrote, taught, and published; received prizes and fellow-
ships at the highest levels; went to dinner with the great and
the near-great; was invited to all the parties that mattered.
He also married four times, and had many affairs. Life
should have felt rewarding—but it didn't. The parties he

went to bored him; the women he slept with left him wanting; the men whose respect he most desired he felt ignored by.

For most of his eighty-odd years, Alfred Kazin was eaten alive by his own demons. Some who are being eaten alive withdraw into brooding silence; some cry aloud to the heavens. Kazin was distinctly of the second type. Explosive and confrontational, known for what he himself called his ghetto manners, he seemed a man in a perpetual state of high-level anxiety: he envied the success of others; experienced his own talent as insufficient; felt romantically short-changed; obsessed over his Jewishness; and, until the very end, was haunted by the conviction that somewhere a marvelous party was going on to which he had not been invited. None of these neurotic postures found their way into Kazin's work—criticism and autobiography written with great skill and undeniable talent, and in the king's English—but they dominated his inner life to a stunning degree, and the expressiveness with which he continued, throughout his years, to describe private unhappiness informs the bulk of *Alfred Kazin's Journals.*

Kazin kept this journal for more than fifty years; in its entirety, we are told, it runs to more than 7,000 pages. During good times and bad, he turned to it for the comfort and clarification of committing to paper his own impassioned take on daily existence. In time, he came to consider the journal a major enterprise. Although he loved writing criticism, it had never ceased to amaze him that he had not turned out a poet or a novelist. The writing in the journal began to seem similar to the writing that flows from the imagination. In the journal itself he refers repeatedly to the act of keeping it; announcing to himself what it is for, what it will accomplish. He imagined the journal fashioning itself into a metaphoric account of experience—his own and that of his time—written by a man of anguished spirit and sentient intelligence, struggling to make a moral being of himself in the midst of social disorder.

In short: the journal was to be redemption through the making of literature. However obscure such ambitions might have been, Kazin must have entertained the secret thought that this private writing had the makings of a *Herzog* or a *Portnoy's Complaint*—because he repined for years over not being able to get it published in his lifetime; a wish that, thankfully, went unfulfilled. If this journal had been published as is while Kazin lived, in all probability none of his acquaintances would again have spoken to him, as nearly everyone who crossed his path is trashed again and again. The irony here is that everyone he knew was doing the same in *his* diary.

"What a neurotic set we all are," Kazin wrote in 1964 of his generation of Jewish American writers. "[It's] our manners. There is no tradition of self-restraint, of true politeness and inquiry . . . there is no ground on which we do not think we have a right to intrude our clamorous demand."

It isn't that Kazin doesn't sound like Herzog or Portnoy when he talks like this; he does. He, like they, can go on complaining forever about being Jewish, not receiving recognition, needing to get laid—but sounding like Herzog the character, and producing *Herzog* the novel, are not the same. In *Herzog*, Herzog himself becomes a metaphor. It is the rare journal that can do the same for its protagonist, even if the personality of the journal keeper is as complicated as Kazin's.

Two elements dominate the *Journals*: the ongoing grievance of feeling forever left out, and a passion for writing that promises repeatedly to save the diarist from himself. There are, of course, entries here and there about politics, literature, the idea of America; New York intellectuals, women and career, the Brooklyn of his childhood; but for the most part, the book is a remarkably faithful record—kept day after week after month after year—of the extremity of these emotional preoccupations. At times it seems as though Kazin's entire life is composed only of the meanest or the most exalted of impulses, each competing endlessly for his inner attention.

Kazin is psychologically savvy about his own inability to let go of the grievance—nevertheless, he cannot. Over a period of fifty years, it marches on, as strong and demanding at the end as at the beginning. Here's a sample:

1948: "My craving for fame, prestige, 'love', seems uncontrolled . . . I could weep when I realize how much time I waste . . . occupied day in and day out, hour by hour, by my anxiety, my useless shadow-boxing with the imaginary censure and rejection by others . . ."

1955: "[M]y constant feeling of being isolated and of not being a recognizable part of any literary tendency . . . I feel that I do not belong to any of it . . . that I am not classified or classifiable, that I do not belong as a 'writer' or as an abstract 'critic' either and so tend to hug my ideas, fancies, my very love, until they feel like grievances."

1959: "The day so hot, my heart so heavy . . . It seems to me that I am still looking for a position, a philosophy, which will help to escape . . . this rawness, this sensitivity, this eternal cry for love and warmth and security . . ."

1980: "I am haunted by Isaiah Berlin, the Court Jew who always knew everybody at the top and still makes me quiver with resentment when I think of the snubbing I received from his unseeing back at the Santa Caterina Amalfi [Hotel] in 1947."

1982: "So what does this anxious sleeper brood over in the infamous watches of the night? Why he is not more famous, not a 'celebrity' like Other People."

1986: "I shiver when I read day after day of my journal and come across the same anger, the same unappeasability, the same heart, the same unrest and anxiety—a hungry soul, often a bitter soul . . . Still, there is a gnawing loneliness, a sense of living apart . . . And the worst of it is how I resent the social gift in others . . . [the] talent for sociability that I certainly lack. And it makes me bitter, bitter."

At the same time, he loved writing—the act of it, the joy of it—with a singleness of heart that produced both eloquence and wisdom. He loved it because writing was his work. To lose oneself in one's work, he knew early, was to find oneself. This he had known since he had realized that *his* work, in particular, entailed giving shape and depth to his own experience: an awesome task.

"Fidelity to one's own experience," he wrote at the age of thirty-two, "is the most difficult, not the easiest, thing for a writer to practice—it necessitates a real understanding and acceptance of one's own singularity, one's special fate—an ability to separate what we learn from others, from the temptation to hide ourselves under the mask of others . . ."

That same year he also saw that the writer was not working in a vacuum; part of the work included making vital connection with the reader: "The value of a critic can be defined by the extent to which he remembers that he is a reader and by his cleverness and passion in applying that remembrance to the service of his readers." Again, not a thing easily accomplished.

Insight follows insight:

1954: "My greatest problem is in realizing the limits of my subject . . . I am constantly trying to put everything I am and everything I think into a book, and it takes me years to realize just what I can make a book of."

1955: "[I]t is exactly in proportion to [the] full concentration of all our powers on an object—a subject—that the real work is done . . ."

1957: "Only the passionate encounter between the writer and the book makes for real criticism—for the constant sense of new *discovery*. It is the *voyage of discovery* that counts, this passionate journey of perception that counts; the freedom and speculative richness of the discovering mind that counts . . ."

1960: "This is the beauty of writing, of thinking. Every day my cup runs over. I have so many perceptions. They bombard me. I have only to wait for them. How with this gift, my gift, can one be unhappy? What fortune for me. What daily bliss! It suddenly came over me, lifting the fog of the usual self-pity, Great God, Good God, how can one be unhappy when I can think so well every day?"

Entries like these are a powerful reminder of all the good writing—as a critic and a biographer—that this permanently agitated man left behind when he died.

Kazin wrote at least three marvelous memoirs—*A Walker in the City, Starting Out in the Thirties, New York Jew*—all of them first-rate in their richness of detail, evocation of time and place, and fullness of the company with whom the narrator interacts. It is interesting to note, that while many of Kazin's contemporaries—Irving Howe, Lionel Trilling, Daniel Bell—appear in the journals as well as in the memoirs, in the journals all meet uniformly with negative treatment of an often coarse nature. In the memoirs the sense of insult is much reduced by virtue not only of the elegance of the writing, but the writer's intention to rise above narrow self-interest. Again, a genuine accomplishment.

In the autobiographies, Alfred Kazin becomes a narrator whose major concern is with storytelling; the storytelling voice delivers a life set fully in its times. In writing them, Kazin came to understand what every good memoirist understands: that the writer's own ordinary, disheveled, everyday self must give way to that of a narrating self— a self who will tell the story that needs to be told; this narrator—or rather, persona—will simultaneously be both the reason for the story and the servant of the story. In 1964, while teaching himself to do this work, Kazin wrote in his journal:

Basically every autobiography hangs on the value, or impersonation, given to the Me. The Me becomes the central myth, the corridor down which all other characters walk and what counts for the book is simply what single myth or interpretation the author of the recital is willing to give his Me, which one he will choose out of the many selves he really experiences in his daily life.

In Kazin's journals is the richly unmediated expressiveness from which the memoirs derive. That expressiveness is both a glory and a source of dismay. On the one hand, it echoes brilliantly the collective mindset of all those fictional Jewish American narrators whose breast-beating hungers produced culture-changing prose in the '50s and '60s. On the other, it lays bare the appalling nature of raw material untransformed by art. Taken all in all, this book is a remarkable demonstration of how good writing struggles to emerge from the inner chaos with which we all live and that only a writer as talented as Alfred Kazin can bring to its knees.

3

Herman Melville

A recent review in the *Times Literary Supplement* of a new
edition of *Grimm's Fairy Tales* predicted that the book
would fill "a yawning gap," as it rescued the fairy tales from
children and folklorists in order that we, the common
reader, might see the collection as a major literary work. I
read this interesting, pertinent sentence over someone's
shoulder, while sitting on a plane, just as I was about to
open Andrew Delbanco's new biography of Herman
Melville. Surely, the book in my lap would be setting out to
do the same: rescue the author of *Moby-Dick* from the miles
of scholarship informed by the received wisdoms that
surround Melville's life and work, thus making the great
nineteenth-century writer live anew for the current generation of readers.

Herman Melville was born in 1819 in New York City
into a family of social connection and financial failure: the

mother was a Gansevoort, both grandfathers were Revolutionary War heroes, and the father died a bankrupt when Herman was twelve years old, leaving a wife and eight children to struggle on as best they could. None of the children grew up to be what is commonly called successful. Herman went to school now and then; clerked now and then; considered surveying now and then. In the same aimless way, at the age of twenty-one he signed on as a common seaman on a whaling ship from which, after eighteen months at sea, he deserted in the Marquesan Islands, where he was held for some weeks by a native tribe in what he later called "indulgent captivity." Upon his escape, he slowly made his way back to America, now in possession of the experience on which his deepest self would draw for the next fifty years. He'd been gone four years.

He decided to write a book about life among the Polynesian islanders. The book was called *Typee* and it achieved a commercial success that, for a minute, made Melville a minor celebrity; more important, it made him realize that he was a writer. Within the next five years, he turned out four books—*Omoo, Mardi, Redburn, White-Jacket*—each less well received than the one before. One by one, the books moved further away from the simple adventure tale with which he had begun, but the readers of *Typee* did not follow.

Writing had released in Melville a passionate, brooding nature that turned ever more inward, puzzling openly over the concern that had been pressing on him since he'd gone to sea, namely, the metaphysical truth of human existence.

As Babbalanja says in *Mardi*, "I am intent upon the essence of things, the mystery that lieth beyond . . . that which is beneath the seeming." What tormented men, Melville had come to realize, was not so much the longing to believe that there is meaning in the universe as the suspicion that behind the longing lies the fear of nothingness. At sea he had watched both the longing and the fear play themselves out fully—seen the ongoing struggle in those around him between the potential for savagery and the need for transcendence—and he'd come to understand that the behavior Christians call civilized does not reach down to the center. Given the right circumstances, most men can demonstrate that both Good and Evil are conditional, and that the elemental forces of life are overwhelming. Wherefore, then, God and Satan?

The question obsessed him. There developed within him a moodiness that William James would trace to "the craving of the heart to believe that behind nature there is a spirit whose expression nature is." As this craving could not be satisfied, it haunted him. Years after they'd met, Hawthorne, during a visit with Melville in Liverpool, wrote in his journal: "It is strange how he persists . . . in wandering to-and-fro over these [theological] deserts . . . He can neither believe, nor be comfortable in his unbelief, and he is too honest and courageous not to try to do one or the other . . . he has a very high and noble nature, and better worth immortality than the rest of us."

For the readers of *Typee*, each new literary offering of Melville's seemed a cheat. These morbid, confused abstractions were not what they had signed on for—and, indeed, the narrative line in these books is often bogged down as Melville struggles to clarify what compels him yet resists his control. He knew he was alienating his readership—"If doubts distract you," says a character in *Mardi*, "in vain will you seek sympathy from your fellow men"—but what could he do other than become his own searching self?

In the spring of 1850, Melville sat down to write just one more tale of whaling ships and the men who work them, but this one overtook him as none before it had.

Suddenly everything came together—language, structure, metaphor—with extraordinary multiplicity; one story, as he said later, turned out to be two, the larger of which drank his blood, while the other demanded only his ink. Here, at last, he knew what he was doing—and what he was doing was writing a major contribution to American literature in a Modernist style that would not come into its own for another hundred years. The book, of course, was *Moby-Dick;* and it was (famously) as great a critical and commercial failure as his other books had been. Only a handful of people—among them Hawthorne—saw *Moby-Dick* for the masterwork that it was.

Melville kept on writing—poems, stories, novels, among them *Pierre, Bartleby,* and, at the last, *Billy Budd*—but the forty years after *Moby-Dick* (he died in 1891) constituted something of a life sentence: the long, painful years of a failed writer living in depressed and reclusive obscurity, working in the New York Customs House, seeing almost no one, entirely forgotten by whatever public he had once had. Upon his death many were surprised to learn that Melville had still been alive.

Oh yes, one other thing: he was married for more than forty years to a woman of his own class with whom he had two sons and two daughters, but neither in his wife nor in any of his children did Melville find a soulmate. Nowhere at home did he receive solace of the spirit, find relief from or exaltation in that which pressed so sorely on him. Perhaps it was this unhappy circumstance that turned the impassioned and volatile writer into a stricken domestic tyrant who stormed about the house, frightening all who came his way, then dissolving in bitter regret. For years on end the family, according to Melville's granddaughter, suffered "not only from insufficient funds for daily needs but far more from his bursts of nervous anger and attacks of morose conscience." One son committed suicide at eighteen, the other died at thirty-five far from home.

For some contemporary readers, this dramatic failure of domesticity is added proof of Melville's homoerotic leanings. I say "added" because much has also been made of his extravagant unhappiness over Hawthorne's willingness to let their friendship drift (in a letter Melville writes bitterly that Hawthorne "withholds" himself, and in a poem he seems to beg the older writer, "Give me yourself!"). But, above all, it has been argued, it is in the writing itself that the homoerotic Melville is inescapably to be found: in the extraordinary portraits of male companionship (Ishmael and Queequeg in *Moby-Dick*), the clear adoration of male beauty (*Billy Budd*), the erotic cast of men in bondage to one another (*Benito Cereno*). One could easily go on and on. But what, exactly, are we to make of that which is clearly there for all to read?

For me, Melville's homoeroticism is akin to that of D. H. Lawrence. They were two men who hungered to reach down to the very center of human existence where the self that was dark, free, wild, even mystic—have I left out any piece of the rhetoric? —was waiting to be discovered. Both wanted to know, with an almost religious hysteria, the primitive "truth" of things more deeply than either wanted anything else. Each writer associated such knowingness entirely with the world of men; the world of strong and vivid action; the one in which one came dangerously up against one's own fears and desires. It was only with men that one could get naked, so to speak. With women one was always somehow clothed. In their world there was the relief of order, sentiment, convention; but here one struggled incessantly against the constraint that domesticity placed on inner exploration.

Yet each man was ineluctably attached to women—clung to them, wouldn't have known how to put it together without them—at the same time that he eroticized in imagination if not in actuality (the truth we'll never know) what passed between men. In short, whether he understood it or not, each felt the amazing complexity of sexual force— and it was out of what he felt that he wrote. The genius lay in the strength of sensibility.

It seems to me that these are the complications we are calling homoerotic, and they are interesting when seen in the light of a psyche divided in anguish and excitement against itself, rather than that of straightforward sexual attraction to the members of one's own sex. This self-division is, in fact, the key which, when turned, opens the door—in Melville as well as in Lawrence—to the inner drama out of which both made great fiction.

During most of the century and more since Melville's death, a mountain of American scholarship—some glorious, most mundane—has accumulated around his work and his person. Among the more luminous of the critical works is F. O. Matthiessen's 1941 classic, *American Renaissance: Art and Expression in the Age of Emerson and Whitman*, a book that many consider the seminal text in American literary studies. The book is inspiring not only for the freshness of Matthiessen's insights into nineteenth-century American writing, but for the remarkable sensitivity with which he writes. In a discussion of *Moby-Dick* Matthiessen tells us, "The instinctive rightness with which [Melville] interrelated the levels of his structure can be seen only by a kind of slow moving-picture of the whole"—and then proceeds to give us this "slow moving-picture" so beautifully the reader could weep. Here we have the kind of absorptive, hovering prose that makes literature out of criticism.

The work done on Melville the man is, I think, often more problematic. Every biographer begins by complaining that the subject is "unknowable," as a vital absence of documentation surrounds the life, and then proceeds to churn out hundreds and hundreds of pages that, in the end, seem to confirm the original misgiving. Within the past ten years alone we have had Hershel Parker's two-volume biography—nearly two thousand pages long!—at the end of which many readers have felt that they do not know Melville any better than they did before they read the biography; while everything about him is on the page, the man himself remains elusive.

Oddly enough, upon the appearance of the first volume of the Parker biography it was Andrew Delbanco, professor of American Studies at Columbia, who wrote, in an unusually lengthy essay in the *New York Review of Books*, "Herman Melville is a singularly unyielding subject for literary biography," as "the dim record of Melville's life simply disappears into the glare of his work, and the best one can hope for is to glimpse a few moments of convergence between them." Essentially, the review accused Parker of having turned a "digitized log into a biography" marked by the kind of "promiscuous detail" that spoke to an academic thesis both reductive and overdetermined. Curiously enough, the overdetermined thesis was that of sexual longing—"at the root of every mood and motivation [Parker finds] sexual craving"—and it wasn't that Delbanco thought there was no truth in this observation, only that in Parker's hands it became an axe that the hapless biographer ground relentlessly because he had no real ideas. There was, in Delbanco's view, "no grand theme" emerging from Parker's lifelong literary devotion.

Now here we are, eight years later, with Delbanco himself weighing in with four hundred–odd pages on the man he long ago told us was a bad bet for literary biography. The reader cannot help wondering, *So why write another one?* And, as though hearing the silent question, Delbanco replies, but in terms that seem to this reviewer something less than reassuring. "The reason," he confides in his preface, "has to do with a feeling that we all live by some unknowable combination of free will and fate. This feeling tends to grow as one gets older, and so there is a certain comfort in watching someone make something beautiful and enduring out of the recalcitrance and fleetingness of life." There is a sense of the reverential in this abstraction that grows even stronger when Delbanco "shares" with us the memory of a time when he held an old letter of Melville's in his hands and felt that he was "eavesdropping, like a tourist in a church who comes upon a worshipper kneeling in prayer." Now we know we are in the presence of adoration; and sure enough, the preface ends with "Anyone who reads Melville's words will know what Emerson meant when he wrote in his journal that, while reading Shakespeare, "I actually shade my eyes.""

These sentences, I must admit, made me desperately uncomfortable. What, I wondered, can follow from such a beginning, except hagiography, pure and simple. The thought proved both warranted and unwarranted: Delbanco's book is hagiography, though not pure and simple.

Melville: His World and Work is a full and faithful account of all that is already known and recorded of the writer's personal life, and it places that life richly (and again, fully) in the politics and culture of its century-spanning time. Delbanco has, of course, read everything by and about his subject and can—and does—rehearse a wealth of responses to Melville's work. On the one hand, this rehearsal demonstrates the authority of research; on the other, it gives us a book saturated in quotations from other readers. On every other page—or so it seems—Lewis Mumford notes, Elizabeth Hardwick observes, Harold Bloom remarks. A rudimentary list of those quoted includes Edward Said, Walker Percy, E. M. Forster, Newton Arvin, Edmund

Wilson, W. H. Auden, John Updike, along with the lesser known but influential academics Frank Lentriccia, Richard Slotkin, and Dominic La Capra. The odd thing here is that much of what these scholars and writers say can be said without the invocation of their illustrious names; for example: as Elizabeth Hardwick remarked, the man who wrote *Typee* was not "a painter of his own face in the mirror"; as Lewis Mumford observed, in New York Melville "simply could not forget the wideness of the world"; as Slotkin has said, Moby Dick is "at once masculine and feminine, a phallus and an odalisque."

Now, Delbanco is a sophisticated writer who could easily have put these sentiments into words of his own. Yet he chose not to. Not, I think, out of the ordinary academic habit of piling up superficial appeals to authority, but rather because he is intent on creating a brilliant surround for the work of a writer whom he does, in fact, love indiscriminately; one that is meant to draw us irresistibly inside the persuasion that Melville's work is not only majestic but inordinately protean: it can and does mean all things to all persons in all times, accommodating itself easily to whatever system of interpretation the cultural moment brings into focus. That, I think, is the thesis to which this biography is dedicated.

Thus, we have quotes to support the suggestion of a transcendental Melville, a Modernist Melville, a Cold War Melville, a gay Melville, an ecological Melville, a Melville of American imperialism and of anti-imperialist blowback. This last, in particular, gets a great deal of play. Edward Said is quoted as having said, on the eve of the Afghanistan invasion, "Collective passions are being funneled into a drive for war that uncannily resembles Captain Ahab in pursuit of Moby-Dick", and Delbanco helps him out by observing that, later, many others "likened President Bush to Ahab in his determination to attack Iraq." This book was published before Denis Donoghue ventured that *Moby-Dick* foretold America's bid for global domination, but not before Delbanco could tell us that the *Pequod* is really the Democratic Party of 1850 falling to pieces.

But it is when we read, "The binary balance of [Melville's] sentences creates a seesaw feeling not very different from what one feels when reading a late twentieth-century postmodern writer like Jacques Derrida or Paul de Man" that we know we are in the presence of a writer whose claims for his subject are so far-reaching as to lose their interpretive value, and we cannot help wondering, *What is going on here?* Where is the "grand theme" that holds all this indiscriminate theorizing together? Merely to ask the question is to answer it.

The problem is one of imagination. When F. O. Matthiessen presented Melville in the truly grand terms by which we have considered him for fifty years—the tragic vision of Man Against Nature, our own Innate Depravity, the guilty need for Crucified Innocence, the Malign Intelligence of existence itself—those terms were fresh, original, exhilarating. Today they are worn thin, in criticism and biography alike. On the other hand, the simple substitution of newer terms derived from Freud, politics, and literary theory are equally unsatisfying—reductive and schematic— when applied by scholars working within a mental framework derived from academic conventions that do not allow the subject to fly free. Delbanco's book is neither reductive nor schematic—it is well written and, more importantly, strongly engaged—yet it does not, cannot, bring us Melville anew because in the deepest sense it is hemmed in by these very conventions.

What is needed for a figure as iconized as Melville is a biographer possessed by a flash of original insight around which the "life" can be organized, the kind that is very little dependent on documentation. The only obligation of such insight is that it prove genuine not fabricated, and that it deepen the writing until something true about the man who wrote *Moby-Dick* is acutely felt by responsive readers who are sure to recognize the close of a yawning gap when they see one.

4

Kathleen Collins

A master of the short story that is all voice, Grace Paley was famous for having come down against the fiction of plot and character development because, as she once said, "Everyone, real or invented, deserves the open destiny of life." In Paley's stories the narrating voice—urban, ethnic, rooted in lived experience—is most often speaking directly to the consequences of that open destiny which, once pursued, never fails to take its toll. In one Paley story the narrator runs into her ex-husband whom she cheerfully addresses as "Hello, my life," but then has an exchange with him that reminds her that "He had had a habit throughout the twenty-seven years of making a narrow remark which, like a plumber's snake, could work its way through the ear down the throat, halfway to my heart. He would then disappear, leaving me choking with equipment."

The voice that speaks those sentences becomes the story being told. Its every inflection deepens and enriches the Paley persona that incarnates the wisdom of Paley the writer: namely, that women and men remain longing, passive creatures most of their lives, always being acted upon, only rarely acting themselves. At its most distilled, this wisdom achieves the lucidity of the poet; or even that of the visual artist. I've often thought of Paley's sentences as the equivalent of color in a Rothko painting. In Rothko, color is the painting; in Paley voice is the story.

Kathleen Collins, an American writer who died in 1988 at the age of forty-six, leaving behind a trunkful of unpublished manuscripts—stories, plays, a journal, an unfinished novel—was a natural at this kind of writing. Now, nearly thirty years after her death, sixteen of the stories found in that trunk have been published as a collection called *Whatever Happened to Interracial Love?* In all of them we hear a voice—black, urban, unmistakably rooted in lived experience—speaking not only to let us know what it felt like to be living inside that complex identity, but to make large, imaginative use of it, the way Grace Paley used her New York Jewishness, to explore the astonishment of human existence.

She was born in 1942 in Jersey City, New Jersey, into a middle-class black family—her father was a state legislator—as conscious of class as it was of race. She was educated at Skidmore College where she majored in philosophy and religion. In 1961 she joined a summer project to help build a youth center in a village in the Congo, and the following year went south with SNCC to help register black voters. However, she proved not to be an activist. In 1963 she went to Paris where she received an MA in French literature and cinema studies at the Sorbonne; when she came back to New York it was to join the faculty at City College of New York as a teacher of film history and screenwriting.

Very soon she began making films of her own, as well as writing plays and stories. A number of these plays were produced to a fair amount of acclaim, and the most distinctive of her films, *Losing Ground,* was only in 2016 restored and reissued. Somewhere in the middle of all this she married, had two children, and by the mid-1970s had endured a painful divorce that became the inspiration for some of her most evocative pieces of prose. A week after her second marriage in 1987 she was diagnosed with breast cancer and within the year she was dead. None of her stories were published in her lifetime.

The writer upon whom Kathleen Collins consciously modeled herself was the playwright Lorraine Hansberry, who wanted to use her blackness to make the women and men in her audience feel as trapped as did her various characters in the existential free fall of ordinary everyday despair—poverty, loneliness, ill health—compounded by the despair of having been born into the wrong sex or race or class.

Whatever Happened to Interracial Love? is, deliberately I presume, so arranged that it is not until the fourth story that the reader realizes the writer is both black and a woman. This arrangement—made, no doubt, by a clever editor—reflects a developing perspective that not only binds the pieces together into a book, it tells us how to read the book. Sometimes the narrating voice is that of a woman, sometimes a man; sometimes it speaks in the first person, sometimes in the third. And quite often it adopts the convention of poetic repetition. No matter: at all times it is distinguished by a similarity of tone and temperament (calm, measured, above all unsurprised) and an unwavering interest in looking as long and as hard as it can at what is, and what is not. Taken all in all, this voice develops into a persona that is striking for the sheer richness of its human presence.

The opening stories are two sets of monologues on the exquisite pain of failed love, the first being given by an unidentified film director ostensibly instructing a cameraman (or woman) on how to light a movie being made about a break-up; the second is shared by a husband and wife, each reporting separately on their long estrangement. Here are the director's words in abbreviated form:

> Okay, it's a sixth-floor walk-up, three rooms in the front, bathtub in the kitchen, roaches on the walls . . . Okay, let's light it for night. I want a spot on that big double bed that takes up most of the room . . . Good. Now let's have a nice soft gel on the young man composing his poems or reading at his worktable. And another soft one for the young woman standing by the stove killing roaches . . . Now backlight the young woman as she lifts that enamel counter covering the bathtub and put a little light on him undressing her and a nice soft arc on the two of them nude in the doorway. Nice touch . . . Now

dim the light. No, take it way down. She looks too anxious and sad. Keep it down. He looks too restless and angry. Down some more . . . She's just waiting at the window. No, on second thought, kill it, he won't come in before morning . . . Now find a nice low level while they're lying without speaking. No kill it, there's too much silence and pain. Now fog it slightly when he comes back in the evening, and keep it dim while they sit on the bed. Now how about a nice blue gel when he tells her it's over. Good. Now go for a little fog while she tries not to cry. Good. Now take it up on him a little while he watches her coldly, then up on her when she asks him to stay. Nice. Now down a bit while it settles between them and keep it down while he watches her, just watches her, then fade it to black, and leave her in the shadow while she looks for the feelings that lit up the room.

Here are the husband and wife:

Husband: It's a long improvisation, my life . . . I was never a pleasure to have around . . . I'm moody, dammit, and restless . . . and life has so many tuneless days . . . I can't apologize for loving you so little . . . I love everything too little, except the journey, the way the wheels turn . . . you accommodated yourself instantly to all my whims . . . fancying them into significant escapades of the soul . . . while . . . I won't apologize for loving you so little . . . no woman living has ever been part of my dreams . . . and life has so many tuneless days.

Wife: The first time my husband left me, I took a small cabin in the woods . . . I was going to stay the whole summer. I stayed three days . . . I came back home . . . it was very hot and lonely . . . I took to crossing the Brooklyn Bridge in the evenings at the time the sun was setting . . . I took to reading memoirs . . . it was one of my finer moments when I discovered that no human life escapes the tribulation of solitude . . . the summer grew hotter and lonelier . . . I began to feel I was drying out inside . . . it encouraged me to consider a little light fucking . . . he turned out to be tall, fervently sincere behind thick bifocals . . . and with a penis about the size of a pea . . . I took it as an omen that I was not designed for light fucking . . . Winter came . . . I rode the subway to Coney Island. The cold, lonely stretch of beach, the abandoned amusement park . . .

And that was just the first time he left her.

In the third story the word "negro" appears for the first time, and then almost casually:

I had an uncle who cried himself to sleep. Yes, it's quite a true story and it ended badly. That is to say, one night he cried himself to death. He was close to forty . . . He was quite handsome. Negro. But a real double for Marlon Brando . . . It is difficult to separate this story from the slight props of race necessary to bolster it up. I have said he was Negro . . . In the middle of the night he began to cry . . . How he could cry! Give in to his crying, allow it full possession of his being as if life were a vast well of tears and one must cry to the center of it . . . It was surely perverse, surely bound to the color of his skin . . . He utterly honored his sorrow, gave into it with such deep and boundless weeping that it seemed as I stood there that he was the bravest man I had ever known.

When it comes to women and men together, Collins is often at her most playful, making the hunger for sexual experience seem as comical as, at other times, it is painful. In one story a college student riffs on the beautiful black activist whom she has settled on as the appropriate person to rid her of her virginity. Something, it turns out, easier said than done. Charlie Jones is light-skinned, green-eyed, and a freedom rider. Our narrator knows, she just *knows,* that he is the right person to initiate her. But then, to her amazement, Charlie seems unable to get the job done. Push, the narrator tells him, push hard. He's got to be the right person, he's just got to be. Push, Charlie Jones, push. Yes, ma'am, says Charlie. But at last:

"Charlie Jones."

"Yes, ma'am . . ."

"It won't go in . . ."

"No, ma'am . . ."

"Not even with your green eyes . . ."

"No, ma'am . . ."

"And your extra-light skin . . ."

"No, ma' am . . ."

"And your freedom riding . . ."

"No, ma'am . . ."

"I guess you're not the right person . . ."

It is in the title story that we get the clearest exposition of the life and times within which the guiding sensibility behind these stories is to be found. Here, the time is 1963, the place an Upper West Side apartment shared by two young women, one "negro," as Collins has it, the other "white." Both are just out of college, both deep into civil rights, and both determinedly in love with young men of the opposite race: the white woman with a black poet who seems never to leave the apartment, the black with a white freedom rider who keeps getting his jaw broken in Mississippi.

The narrating point of view, delivered in the third person, is that of the black roommate who is struggling to understand what she is living through, even as she sympathizes with the feelings of her dangerously disappointed parents, members of the black bourgeoisie who are watching everything they've worked for disintegrate before their eyes: "Their sons [and daughters] will go to jail for freedom (which in their parents' minds is no different from going to jail for armed robbery, heroin addiction, pimping, and other assorted ethnic hustles)." Nonetheless, the young woman is writing to her father,

Daddy, you must see that I must lead my own life even if you don' t understand it and all this talk about color all the time. I'm not the same anymore and I have to be what I am. I've lived with all kinds of people . . . and now I'm trying to live with some white people and some "negro" people and find out who I am and I have to do it and . . .

But then, life being what it is, even in "the year of race-creed-color blindness," as she sits writing this letter the doorbell rings, and there on the threshold stands her lover, the freedom fighter who had wanted desperately to marry her, crying. "He had something to say: He had just come from his parents' house. He knew now that he could not marry her. He knew now that he would never go back south. It was all over. He understood now that he could never be" the Negro he had wanted to be for her. "Never. Ever. And then he was gone." The young woman closes the door thinking she must get another apartment, one where she will be able to "think and see clearly, about how integration came into style. And people getting along for a while. Inside the melting pot. Inside the melting pot." The last line of the story is "It's 1963. Whatever happened to interracial love?"

Only rarely again in this book will the narrating point of view sound as young as it does in this story; and never again will it sound accommodating. The measured voice now complicates itself—there's iron in it—as more and more it begins to record the slights and humiliations and knife thrusts that continually push the born outsider to the limits of endurance.

In "Only Once," a short, incantatory tale, a woman remembers an affair with an irresistible daredevil. "He had to execute a perfect jump," she tells us. The man was forever prancing about on the top of the Brooklyn Bridge or preparing to jump off a rock the size of a boulder or leap across the third rail, always calling out to the narrator, "Think I can make it?" And grinning:

Like he could open and close life. With his laughing eyes. Poised. And his golden body. Poised.

She didn't want to watch. Not this time. Nor any of the other times. "Only once do you know that kind of man, they say. Only once."

Then one day,

He didn't clear the rail. Or maybe he did. Maybe it was later. He mistimed a dive from a high cliff. Or maybe he didn't. Maybe it was even later than that. He shot himself in the head. Thought the gun was empty. Or maybe he knew it wasn't.

Only once do you know that kind of man, they say. Only once. But she would know them all her life. One after the other they would turn out to be that kind of man.

No surprises here. Shocks perhaps, but not surprises.

The narrator in this story is giving us a view of an inner reality she and the daredevil are equally intimate with. It's as if they had both grown up confined by the accident of skin color to a narrowness of experience that resembles living under house arrest. They both know every inch of their restricted territory by heart; and if content to keep their heads down and remain well within its bounds, never seeking to break out into the world beyond, they could perhaps get by as anonymous survivors of the raw deal into which they have been born. The woman, conceivably, is willing to do so; the man is not. He is compelled to risk self-destruction rather than forget that promise of an open destiny that imagined others seem to share. And she? What is she compelled to do? Stand witness.

What we have here, in Collins's sixteen stories, is sensibility in service to a state of mind whose authenticity none, I think, can challenge. Written in the 1970s and '80s, when African-American writing was ablaze with rage and righteousness, they might have seemed too nuanced to signify. Coming to us as they do now, when we are living once more through a period of flaring racism that has brought talented protest writing to a new level, they strike a note on the one hand oddly original, on the other painfully familiar. Either way it drags at the heart.

5

Diana Trilling

In the 1940s and '50s, when book culture in America was a real presence, Diana Trilling was among the most deliciously feared of literary critics. Today, it is something of a marvel to read her work of those long ago years. The sheer high-handedness of the writing, exhilarating and exasperating as it is, can still put color in the reader's cheek. From the get-go, Trilling is shaking her finger at her subjects. She has a measuring rod in her head that turns on a strict notion—shades of her famous husband, Lionel—of the relation between literature and moral responsibility. If by this standard, the book she is reading is deemed acceptable it gets a nod of approval; if not, off with its head. One critique—which can stand in for a multitude—branded the book under review "a muddled, pretentious, vulgar book, to be noticed in fact only for its indecency."

Books, for Diana, were either decent or indecent, vulgar or civilized, responsible or irresponsible. Forget the hundreds of skewered writers who have gone down into oblivion; routinely, she took apart the likes of John Cheever, Eudora Welty, Evelyn Waugh, Arthur Koestler. Reviewing Truman Capote's debut novel, *Other Voices, Other Rooms*, in 1948, she wrote, "I find myself deeply antipathetic to the whole artistic-moral purpose of Mr. Capote's novel. I would freely trade 80 percent of his technical skill for 20 percent more value in the uses to which it is put." As for Virginia Woolf, Diana sadly informed her readers that "we face the fact that Mrs. Woolf's hand lacks the strength to grip an essential truth." Diana herself loved to repeat the story of an émigré novelist from Nazi Austria who was said to have remarked that while he had lost his home, his country, and his language, he had at least had the good fortune to not be reviewed by Diana Trilling.

The woman who wrote those reviews and repeated that story, it will come as no surprise, was herself the victim of an extraordinary capacity for feeling wounded by others. She kept a running score of who admired or scorned, supported or opposed, denigrated or celebrated her; ascribed all criticism of her work or her person to jealousy or envy; and was certain that at whatever dinner party to which she had not been invited there had been someone plotting to take her down. For more than half of her ninety years she awakened each day to rehearse anew the list of allies and enemies constantly vibrating in her head. Living as she did in an almost entirely male world where she was certainly subjected to the kind of vicious sexism that went routinely unchallenged in those years—the middle decades of the twentieth century—it is yet hard to not conclude that the shape this life took owed much to the kind of inborn emotional grievance—those narcissistic wounds that never close—that no amount of cultural change can ever do away with.

Diana Rubin Trilling was born in 1905 in New York City into a well-to-do family of immigrant Polish Jews where at earliest age she exhibited the contradictions of personality that were to inform her life. To an inordinate degree, the family prized outspokenness—known in some quarters as truth-speaking, in others as confrontation—and the bright young Diana was encouraged to speak her mind boldly and baldly, letting the chips fall where they may. At the same time that this formidable forthrightness was flourishing, there also developed in her—and perhaps the two are destined to go hand in hand—a variety of free-floating anxiety that announced itself first as a fear of the dark, then of heights, then burglars and break-ins, and at last (most dominating of all) a fear being left alone. While this is not at all an unusual combination of personality traits—brash certainty masking unrelieved insecurity—in Diana's case, it proved very nearly debilitating.

The family had money and enough social ambition to send its clever daughter to Radcliffe where, as with most women of her class and generation, she received an education more resembling that of a finishing school than a university. The young women were openly being prepared to become the appropriate mate of a potentially powerful husband: an expectation that seemed eminently reasonable to Diana and one that, in due time, she fulfilled.

In 1927 mutual friends introduced her to Lionel Trilling, a graduate student of her own age, studying for a Ph.D. in literature at Columbia. Not long after they met Lionel wrote in his journal that she "had the mechanical trick of being able to talk about anything," and while "her laugh and her voice irritate me, and her talk does not stimulate but rather represses" he nonetheless found her sexually exciting. They soon fell in love and within the year slept together. "Surely going to bed with a man before marriage was the most courageous act of my life," she later said, and never had reason to amend that assessment.

The Trillings were married in 1929, and remained joined at the hip until Lionel's death in 1975. It seems unlikely that Diana ever slept with another man; nor did Lionel, although he fumbled about a bit, actually sleep with another woman. From all available evidence, the pair remained profoundly ignorant of the contradictory dictates of erotic life when experienced fully, even though both pronounced— and for decades on end—on the human motivation out of which literature of the imagination is made.

Lionel soon became Lionel Trilling—distinguished professor of literature at Columbia University and a major American critic—and Diana the competent, albeit restless helpmeet. She kept house, organized their increasingly busy social life, and took an active hand in aiding her husband with his work. Hungry to think of her life as purposeful, she mentally elevated her job description to "family feminist." Scorning women who wanted to be men, as Clare

Boothe Luce had scorned them in her famous play *The Women*, Diana developed the notion that, as her biographer, Natalie Robins, puts it in *The Untold Journey: The Life of Diana Trilling*, "women in concert with men and their families will transform modern life." A dubious definition of modern feminism, to say the least, and one that in reality ate away at whatever genuine self-regard she might otherwise have attained.

It turned out she was a born editor—someone with a gift for knowing how to transform a clotted sentence into a readable one, and structure a piece of writing so that the thought behind it achieved clarity—but instead of getting a job as one, she devoted herself to cleaning up her husband's writing and, quite early, convinced herself that without her his work would never have been fully realized. She was certain that after Lionel died and his manuscripts went public, her contribution to the famous essays would be made known to the world. But then Lionel did die, and she discovered that he had destroyed all those drafts with her editing notes on them. Distraught is not the word for what she felt. For years afterward, her son, James Trilling, said, "it was the only thing she kept coming back to with sorrow and anger—'how could he do this to me?' "

The reason this particular "betrayal" went deep was that she burned for vindication in the eyes of those high-minded friends and enemies of Lionel's known as the New York Intellectuals—Philip Rahv, Delmore Schwartz, Irving Howe, Dwight Macdonald, need I go on?—the group of critics who occupied a vital place in the literary/political culture of this country between the 1930s and the '70s, and whom Diana (rightfully) thought of as her lifelong detractors. These men were marked by a ferocious devotion to the kind of argument during which you determined not on besting your opponent, but annihilating him. The only women even remotely considered equals at this game were Mary McCarthy and Hannah Arendt; all others were wives or girlfriends who were admitted to social gatherings but never listened to.

Intent on getting her own back, in her 1993 memoir, *The Beginning of the Journey*, Diana characterized the New York Intellectuals as "smug, ungracious, contemptuous, condescending, judgmental, incoherent." Ironically, she failed to recognize that when her turn came, her tongue proved as cutting as theirs, her judgments as absolute, and her insistence on the rightness of her opinions equally as unyielding.

Diana's turn came in 1941, when Lionel recommended her for the position of fiction reviewer at the *Nation*, and she got the job. At long last, she had been provided a platform on which she could speak her mind in print, and a flood of pent-up critical energy was released that abated only with her death. Diana left behind three collections of essays and reviews, a full-length biography, and a memoir: all of which have earned her a place in American literary history. By the late 1940s, Diana had come to consider herself a cultural critic justified in holding public views not only on books, but politics, social trends, movies . . . you name it, she had an opinion on it. In certain cases, it was not just an opinion she held, but an interest so strong it qualified as a defining position. First and foremost, there was communism in America; second, psychoanalysis; third, Lionel's potential to have been a novelist of significance.

Communism in America was the great bugaboo of Diana Trilling's life. From the mid-'30s on, she saw it as a threat to the American democracy worthy of the highest moral outrage. Making no distinction between communists in America and those in the Soviet Union, she described the work of American CP organizers as operating under a "chain of high command" that constituted "the evil within," was bent on "the entrapment of innocents," and was now "drenched through our culture." She often thought it more important to fight this "evil within" than to secure American civil rights, and could truly never understand why this made others see her as a reactionary. To read her today on communism with either a small c or a capital c is jaw-dropping: alternately ludicrous and frightening. Not once in all her red-baiting diatribes does an insight emanate from anything that might resemble an emotional imagination.

Then there was psychoanalysis. Throughout the 1930s and '40s, in perpetual search of a cure for her unabating anxieties, she underwent one form or another of psychotherapy. All in all, there were seven analysts in twenty years—one, as she sniffed, more ignorant than the last—under whose treatment she, by her own account, remained substantially unchanged. Nonetheless, analytic psychobabble became a staple of her conversation with friends and relatives alike. Lionel once told someone that Diana "didn't simply get mad at him; she threw him back into his infancy and psychoanalyzed him." Another friend often begged her to "please take down your shingle" and stop speaking in the "tone of a psychiatrist talking calmly to a lunatic." One might have thought that devotion to analytic insight would produce some understanding of, if not sympathy with, those liberationist movements of the 1970s, especially the women's movement, which clearly originated in, as a wit of the time put it, "one's own hurt feelings." But such was not the case. Like her illustrious husband, Diana was a self-styled nineteenth-century liberal and saw the movement only as disruptive.

And lastly we come to Diana's undying conviction that Lionel could have been a major novelist if only—if only the times had been different, if only he hadn't needed to make a living, if only publishers and editors had been more encouraging. This claim, on the face of it, is absurd. Lionel Trilling longed to be a novelist because for him, as for every artist and intellectual of his generation, the very definition of a writer was one who wrote fiction successfully. But the fact of the matter was he could never put felt life on the page. End of major novelist story. Not, however, for her. Never, for her.

Diana Trilling spent her life declaring that she was her own separate self, but at no time—except when she is pontificating about communism or psychoanalysis—does she imagine herself except in relation to her husband. There are not two pages together, either in her memoir or in the Robins biography, where Lionel is absent. Such an attachment, needless to say, is bound to breed a wealth of negative as well as positive feeling. Thus, while Diana regularly announces that of *course* Lionel is a genius, she just as regularly points out that he can't swim, he can't drive, he can't balance a checkbook; and when she was pregnant he wouldn't come near her. She also reports that Lionel routinely suffered from raging depressions during which—she wonders why—he screamed that Diana had poisoned his very existence.

In its own ironic way, hers is an exemplary life: the life of an intelligent and talented woman who, struggling to achieve an inner sense of worth while spending the majority of her years in the shadow of borrowed glory, became so obsessed with the double bind in which she found herself that ultimately, in her own eyes, it became her inescapable identity. To the very end Diana brooded that the leading line of her obituary would read "Diana Trilling dies at 150. Widow of distinguished professor and literary critic Lionel Trilling." And indeed; mention her name today and three out of four people will ask, "Who's that?" Add that she was the wife of Lionel Trilling and those same people reply with a nod of recognition.

Hers was the fate of the woman who, regardless of what she herself undertakes to do, lives and dies the Wife of the Great Man. In literary history alone, three women who shared this fate come to mind: Jane Carlyle (wife of Thomas), Clover Adams (wife of Henry), Zelda Fitzgerald (wife of F. Scott). Jane was a celebrated diarist, Clover a brilliant conversationalist and letter writer, and Zelda a gifted dancer and the author of a painfully moving novel. It is not at all clear that the inborn talents of these women were necessarily inferior to those of their famous husbands, but it is certainly clear that while the men were obsessively centered in their work the women never were. This perfectly conventional failure to develop the single-hearted motivation required for work of the first order determined all in their lives that was to follow. In the end, Jane Carlyle withered away, Clover Adams committed suicide, and Zelda Fitzgerald lost her reason. Diana Trilling, however, it must be said, went down fighting.

When she was ninety years old, now blind and with just one more year to live, a journalist at the *Boston Globe* wrote a profile of her that included the observation that while Diana's ankles were "bloated pink and painful over the straps of black sandals," she still had "a tongue sharp as a torn tin can." She must have howled like a wounded animal when these words were read out loud to her, then pulled herself together and dictated a letter to the journalist composed of the kind of gorgeously stern rebuke she might have delivered in a book review written fifty years earlier.

6

Mary McCarthy

When my friends and I were in our twenties—this was in the 1950s—we read two writers, Colette and Mary McCarthy, as others read the Bible: to learn better who we were and how, given the constraint of our condition, we were to live. The condition, of course, was that we were young women, and that Marriage and Motherhood determined the territory upon which our battle with Life was expected to be pitched. It was only in the work of Colette and McCarthy—neither on the syllabus of any lit course I ever took—that we saw two gloriously shocking spins put on the narrative which we'd grown up believing to be our destiny.

In neither of these writers did marriage or motherhood figure at all. For Colette, Love with a capital L, as she referred to erotic obsession, was the ultimate experience for a woman. To know passion was the thing; even—or perhaps especially—if it meant the loss of bourgeois respectability; and if, at the end, when youth and beauty were gone, and one was left humiliated by the inability to arouse desire, so be it. One had *lived*. On this score not another living writer, it seemed to us, understood the stakes as well as Colette. Her work sounded depths of understanding that were like nothing we had ever encountered. She alone could make high art out of the dilemma of a woman "in the grip"; elevate Love to the same metaphoric heights that another novelist could reach through the contemplation of God or War.

But Mary McCarthy spoke to another kind of romance alive in us, one closer to the bone; that of seeing ourselves as New Women, independent working girls out in the world, in pursuit of the kind of adventure that would strengthen not deplete us, for we would then be armed with *experience*. In this scenario, sexual love was flatly instrumental, and this too was exciting, as it illuminated a reality many of us were, unwittingly, beginning to inhabit: that of the unexpected setbacks one encountered on the road to experience. Instead of concentrating on the permutations of ecstasy at a high level as Colette did, McCarthy concentrated on the cost of liberated sex: the startling mixture of curiosity, excitement, and dismay that went with *actually* taking off your clothes and lying down with a stranger who was deeply attractive before you made love but afterward left you with the taste of iron in your mouth.

The thing we prized most in McCarthy was the no-holds-barred honesty with which she nailed the situation. In *The Company She Keeps* (her first novel, published in

1942), she gave us a female protagonist in whom we could see ourselves reflected as we were, right then and there. Who among us, in the 1950s, could not identify with Meg Seargent, bold as brass when she meets the Man in the Brooks Brothers Shirt on a train traveling west and then, in the morning, is crawling around on his sleeping car floor, trying desperately to find her second stocking before he wakes up and forces her to face the humiliating complications of casual sex. The scene was so real that readers like me and my friends could only feel redeemed both by its remarkable verisimilitude, and then by the scary brilliance of the prose, edged not in sentiment or social realism but in glittering irony.

It was the irony in McCarthy's writing that carried the day. Inherent in it was a mockery from which no one—not even the protagonist—was safe; but most especially, the men were not safe. What fools McCarthy made of her men! Not knaves, fools. Just to see them so portrayed, lowered into a bath of scorn, was to feel ourselves raised up. It would be twenty years more before we, the young women who read her in the 1950s, would understand why those early McCarthy stories had spoken so directly to us. That cold, hard stare of hers at romantic relations between men and women was soon to be ours, as one by one we had graduated into a world every bit as sexist as hers had been, and it was only now, in the 1970s, that many of us were able to see McCarthy's relentless need to hold her characters up to ridicule as a line of defense equal to that of Clarissa Dalloway's withdrawal from the marital bed.

Mary McCarthy was born in 1912 in Seattle, the eldest in a family of four children. When she was six years old her parents died within days of one another in the 1918 influenza epidemic that killed nearly fifty million people across the globe. The McCarthy children were taken in by their paternal grandparents, and lived for some years in the Midwest under conditions which Mary later insisted, in *Memories of a Catholic Girlhood*, were Dickensian: brutalizing in mind, body, and spirit.

In her teens, Mary was rescued by her maternal grandparents, returned to Seattle, and thereafter lived in an atmosphere of wealth and kindliness that, nonetheless, did little to mitigate the crude lovelessness of those mean Midwestern years. By the time she entered Vassar she was the fully formed person she would be for the rest of her life: beautiful and brilliant, possessed of an eye protected against sentiment coupled with a steel-trap mind and a tongue feared by all who had been at the receiving end of its talented sarcasm, a sarcasm that for some would always be wickedly amusing, for others just wicked. She married straight out of college in 1933, came to live in New York, soon got divorced, rented a tiny apartment in Greenwich Village, and began her life.

McCarthy and her husband (a man of the theater) had met James T. Farrell, then a well-known novelist of the left, and, after her divorce in 1936, it was to Farrell's Sunday open house that she often made her way. Here she met a wealth of interesting people, made connections among those in publishing, and was soon writing book reviews. Within a year her classy, good-looking, frighteningly clever presence was wanted at literary left-wing parties where, as her biographer Carol Brightman tells us, she was introduced to "progressive hosts and modernist hostesses" at whose functions voices rose "in lively controversy over the new play, the new strike, the new Moscow trials, the new abstract show at the Modern Museum."

It was at these parties that she met the men (Phillip Rahv and William Phillips chief among them) who, in 1937, decided to revive the defunct magazine, *Partisan Review,* that had once been the literary arm of the Communist Party. These men were anti-Stalinist Marxists in love with modernism, and bent on defying the CP's primitive understanding of literature as a tool of polemics; they loved Trotsky because he had said that art could best aid the revolution by being true to itself rather than to political correctness; by which was meant the social realism that dominated the fiction of the '30s.

As McCarthy had been heard to denounce Stalinism at one party or another, she was invited to join the staff of the new *Partisan Review.* Taken on as a drama critic, she quickly and joyously found her youthfully fierce writing voice; and her career as a take-no-prisoners writer was launched. Of Maxwell Anderson, a popular left-wing playwright of the time, she did not hesitate to write "Once again he has been inspired by a lofty theme and once again the mediocrity of his talent has reduced it to inconsequentiality." And when Eugene O'Neill's *Iceman Cometh* was being hailed as a remarkable piece of work, she berated O'Neill for his sentimentality in using a bunch of drunks who, in order to deliver the playwright's message, became more and more articulate as the play went on, when everyone knew that alcohol meant the dissolution of personality, not its sharpening.

"From the beginning," Carol Brightman tells us,

> *Partisan Review* was surrounded by the kind of controversy that quickened Mary McCarthy's pulse. She loved the people at the magazine not for their own particular selves but because [in her own words] they were "a self-proclaimed elite whose measure was to be taken not by its nearness to money or to established institutions, including communist institutions, but by its performance as a harbinger of cultural change."

In essence, this meant endless argument, endless theorizing, endless scoring. McCarthy herself held no real position on any of the issues argued. She was never a serious Marxist or modernist, for that matter—but she was serious about being the provocative child at the back of the room announcing the emperor had no clothes; the one who was always pointing out the inconsistent and the meretricious in whatever argument was being held among all these self-importantly serious, mainly Jewish intellectuals.

One among them, however, she *did* love for his very own self: Phillip Rahv. The central figure in this influential little hotbed of intellectual superiority, Rahv held a passionately uncompromising view of what constituted the real thing in literature as in politics. It was the passion behind Rahv's judgments that elevated him to the position of the most feared, and therefore the most respected, of all—editors and writers alike—who encountered him in the flesh. As Elizabeth Hardwick said of him at his funeral, his outstanding characteristic was "a contempt for . . . the tendency to inflate local and fleeting cultural accomplishments. This slashing away at low levels of taste and at small achievements passing as masterly . . . was a crusade some more bending souls might have grown weary of. But he was not ashamed of his extensive 'negativism' and instead went on right up to the end scolding . . . unworthy accommodation" not for the sake of establishing his own authority, but for "the honor and integrity of history itself."

Like all the others at *Partisan Review*, Mary was seriously intimidated by Rahv's intellectual self-confidence, so the only way to even things out was to go to bed with him. Surprisingly, the two fell in love and became a couple, living openly together to the priggish dismay of many of their comrades who, in reality, were as frightened of sex without marriage as any bourgeois or working-class puritan could be—and even more frightened of women. Among men like Delmore Schwartz, McCarthy was roundly condemned as the vamp who had Rahv, the poor fool, in her clutches. When, in 1938, she suddenly and without warning married Edmund Wilson with whom she had secretly been sleeping, the men at *Partisan Review* felt sneeringly vindicated. Rahv himself was stunned.

Marriage to Edmund Wilson provided Mary McCarthy with an experience of major clarification. For one thing, the Jewish intellectuals had been exotics to her, whereas Wilson, for reasons of class and origin, was her familiar; it came as a surprise that in marrying him, as she said in later years, she felt the relief of "coming home." Then again, she was now with a man who was essentially literary not political and when, at Wilson's insistence, she tried her hand at fiction and first shot out of the box came cool, calculating "Cruel and Barbarous Treatment"—the story that would eventually become the startling first chapter in *The Company She Keeps*—she knew that this was where her writing talent best connected. The stories that then began to pour out of her made it icily clear that it was through fiction that she had become and would remain—irresistibly and irrepressibly— a social satirist of the first order.

It is poignant to see that when McCarthy was writing the kind of satire that involved autobiographical characters like Meg Seargent or Martha Sinnott in *A Charmed Life*, a strain of sympathetic regret softened her otherwise uncompromising take on characters whom she mainly presented as the sum of their disabilities. It never occurred to her that the models for her characters, those whom she was presenting as pompous or self-deluded, would see themselves any differently—after all, she was only speaking the self-evident truth—and was always taken aback when they either bellowed like wounded bears at seeing themselves skewered in print, or simply stopped inviting her to their parties. One who bellowed like a bear was Phillip Rahv, who actually thought of bringing suit to prevent the publication in 1949 of *The Oasis*.

The novella tells the story of a group of would-be utopians who, on the eve of the Cold War and just as fear of the Bomb is heating up, gather together to form a cooperative commune that, by its very existence, they think, will lodge a significant protest against the End of the World scenarios that are overtaking the West. The characters were all drawn from McCarthy's professional and social life: the men at *Partisan Review* itself, as well as those who filled the vast, loosely knit world of left-wing sympathizers, bohemians, fellow travelers, and hangers-on in which she moved. Thus we have among the Utopians not only intellectual leaders, but "an assortment of persons of diffuse and uncommitted goodwill, two editors of a national news weekly, a Latinist teacher of boys . . . a trade union publicist, several New York high-school teachers . . . a middle-aged poet . . . an actor and a radio script-writer," as well as their various husbands, wives, and children.

The ideological leanings of the group are divided between the Realists and the Purists, led on the one hand by Will Taub (clearly Phillip Rahv) and on the other by Macdougal Macdermott (even more clearly Dwight Macdonald). But whether Realists or Purists, all take themselves and their enterprise very seriously; above all, they take seriously their own internal divisions. They might not know how to come up with a working definition of social democracy, but they certainly know how to obsess over one another's theoretical differences; informed of the large number of people who are with him, Taub's instinctive response is "Never mind that. Who's against us?" Whatever the issue, the Utopian leaders will show "far less constraint in characterizing the [opinions of their opponents] as childish, unrealistic, unhistorical, etc., than in formulating a rhetoric of democratic ideals." This is the failure of moral imagination in *The Oasis* upon which McCarthy will concentrate her mocking attention.

From the get-go, she taunts the mixed motives and self-deceptions with which the communards arrive in Utopia. Imagining that what they are about to do will provide an example for the world to emulate, they are in fact, each in his or her own peculiar way, more pre-occupied with secret self-regard than with Utopia's large-minded statement of purpose. In the very first para-graph we are told that Mr. and Mrs. Joseph Lockman were the first to arrive in Utopia because "Joe, in real life a diabetic businessman from Belmont, Massachusetts, had spent thirty years beating his competitors to the jump. Joe's intentions toward Utopia were already formidable: honoring its principles of equality and fraternity, he was nevertheless determined to get more out of it than any-body else . . . He intended to paint more, think more, and feel more than his co-colonists . . . He would not have been in earnest about the higher life if he had failed to think of it in terms of the speed-up."

Then, for (sadly) comic relief we have Katy and Preston who, having been married a bare two years, and are ardently of the Purist party, are mainly involved in strategizing their marital misery. Whenever they have an argument Katy instantly goes on an emotional jag that Preston despises, and has never known how to escape; but now, he, "no doubt about it, was taking advantage of the Utopian brotherhood to shut her out from himself." Utopia was giving him "a privacy he had sought in vain during [their] two years of marriage." Katy, in turn, was discovering "that the privacy to make a scene was something she would miss in Utopia . . . Now surrounded by these watchers, she felt deprived of a basic right . . . to behave badly if necessary until [Preston] responded to her grief."

And yet again, there is Taub's sidekick, Harold Sydney (William Phillips): "A clever, fair-minded man, receptive to discussion and argument, he disliked giving pain, and this in conjunction with the doctrine of necessity to which he and his colleagues were wedded, had made him somewhat weak and evasive . . . His flexible mind extended to take in his opponent's position and then snapped back like an elastic, with the illusion that it had covered ground."

It is Joe Lockman who is the cause of the first moral difficulty the Utopians find themselves in. "What!" cries the ever impassioned Macdougal Macdermott, upon learning that Lockman has been admitted to the colony. "The man's a yahoo! Have you people no standards?" When his wife points out that ostracizing Joe would be "an ugly beginning for a community devoted to brotherhood," Macdermott instantly changes course (as he will time and again), announcing her absolutely right, Joe must be admitted to their company. But the argument itself has caused unease. "The incident, in fact, had frightened them a little. They had caught a glimpse of themselves in a mirror, a mirror placed at a turning point where they had expected to see daylight and freedom, and though each of them, individually, was far from believing himself perfect, all had counted on the virtues of others to save them from themselves."

Still, there remains a Kantian puzzle. "Was it to follow then that *anyone* could be admitted to Utopia—a thief, a blackmailer, a murderer? Why not, declared the purists. Impossible, said the realists." The point, thankfully, remains untested. "No murderers or thieves applied, only ordinary people of ordinary B-plus morality, people whose crimes, that is, had been confined to an intimate circle, and who had never injured anybody but a close friend, a relation, a wife, a husband, themselves."

And there we have the brilliant and quite original thesis of *The Oasis:* the people of the ideological left—intellectuals and plebeians alike—imagine themselves moralists of the first order, when they are in fact possessed of only B-plus morality. In the hands of an Edmund Wilson this thesis might have invoked a sense of tragedy; in the hands of Phillip Rahv himself, unmitigated scorn; with Mary McCarthy it becomes an instrument of contemplative ridicule—perhaps the unkindest cut of all.

The reason that Rahv went ballistic when he read *The Oasis* was that McCarthy is caricaturing his own deeply held credo when she tells us that Will Taub's "whole sense of intellectual assurance rested on the fixed belief in the potency of history to settle questions of value . . ." In practice this meant that he allowed "anyone (excluding fascists and communists) the liberty of behaving as ineffectually as he wished. But the right of a human being to *think* that he could resist history, environment, class structure, psychic conditioning was something denied him with all the ferocity of [his] own pent-up nature and disappointed hopes." And then the *coup de grace:* Taub himself had nothing to offer, by way of a concrete proposal, in the matter of how right-minded people were actually to live out their ideals.

The final test for the Utopians, which they fail badly, comes when a strange family starts picking strawberries in their fields and, after speaking reasonably to the poachers and receiving no response, Preston and another colonist, not knowing what else to do, drive them off the land by taking pot shots in the air with a gun filled with blanks. Joe Lockman, of all people, is the one to call them on this appalling solution to the problem with which they thought they had been faced: "'You've done a terrible thing,' he said solemnly, going up to the two young men and putting a hand on the shoulder of each. 'You've driven a man and his family off this property with a gun . . . I never thought this could happen here.'"

McCarthy sums up the incident with "A phase of the colony had ended, everyone privately conceded . . . The distaste felt by some was so acute that they questioned the immediate validity of staying on in a colony where such a thing could take place. The fault, in their view, lay with no single person, but with the middle-class composition of the colony, which, feeling itself imperiled, had acted instinctively, as an organism, to extrude the riffraff from its midst." The mockery ends in self-mockery as one of the Utopians observes, "Nice people like these are always all right, unless you take them off guard."

The Oasis was first published in England in the British magazine *Horizon*. Its English readers, who could easily identify the original of all the major players, roared with laughter (as we would have had the shoe been on the other foot) at this marvelously executed send-up of the American intellectual scene; many American critics, however, pronounced it brilliant but heartless. They were wrong. The book is not heartless. It is not out for blood. True, irony

inevitably means some fundamental sympathy is being withheld; but the irony here is not savage; its deliciously witty
sentence structure is rooted in the heartfelt disappointment
of a moralist whom the reader feels has really wanted the
good (that is, the genuine) in our midst to prevail.

Today, everyone connected with *The Oasis,* including its
author, is long dead and, as the world from which it emerged
is also long gone, the *roman* à *clef* aspect of the novella
seems no longer of consequence. What does remain of
consequence is the moving sense of familiarity with which
we encounter McCarthy's utopians who, decked out in their
all-too-human shortcomings, are *still* hungry to make anew
a world in which we can all be saved from ourselves. Occupy
Wall Street, anyone?

7

James Salter

In an epigraph at the beginning of his new novel, *All That Is*, James Salter announces that he now realizes everything is a dream, the only reality is that which is preserved in writing. If this is true, Salter—the writer if not the man—has a lot to answer for. I have just spent the last few weeks reading a number of his books and it seems to me that if anything is a dream it is the motive force behind the work of this highly acclaimed writer who, for more than forty years, has been producing novels and stories whose style is uniformly praised but whose content is rarely addressed. Salter is now eighty-seven years old, and much to be applauded for his unimpaired love of writing. On the other hand, at this point in his career it is hard to avoid asking: Who is this man, and what is he actually talking about?

‿᎐‿

James Salter was born James Horowitz in 1925 into an upwardly mobile Jewish family. His mother was a beauty and his father a graduate of West Point who attained the rank of lieutenant and then left the military to make a pile in New York real estate development. James grew up in a world of money and glamour, and came of age with the expectation that neither would ever come to an end. But they did. During the Second World War Salter's father was recalled to active duty as a major. Here, in the wartime army, he achieved the unrivaled success that proved his ruination. "When it was over," Salter tells us in his celebrated memoir, *Burning the Days* (1997), "he was never able to fit in again." Peacetime life now seemed prosaic. "It was the grandiose that attracted him. He was operatic. He lived on praise and its stimulus and performed best, only performed, when the full rays were shining on him." All too soon, the money was gone and along with it the never-to-be-forgotten glamour.

At the age of seventeen, James, like his father before him, entered West Point and upon graduation from the academy went into the Army Air Forces, where he developed a love of flying that nothing else in his long life—neither sex nor money nor fame—has ever matched. It was not just the thrill of flying itself ("the imperishability of it, the brilliance"), but the thrill of flying in the military, especially during wartime, that he truly cherished: "the comradeship, the idealism, the youth." It was with joy that he served as a fighter pilot in the Korean War.

Yet in 1957, the thirty-two-year-old flyer left the military, changed his name to Salter, and embarked on the writing life. Since the late '50s Salter has published nine books of fiction and four of nonfiction. Almost all of this work is drenched in an idealizing nostalgia for an elusive "good life"—invariably associated with taste, money, and mythic sex—that, from the beginning, was received with open arms by readers famous and obscure for whom Salter's lush, evocative writing was experienced as haunting.

"It was the autumn of 1958. Their children were seven and five. On the river the color of slate, the light poured down." Thus begins the second chapter of the 1975 novel *Light Years*, tells the story of an apparently magical couple— he's talented, she's beautiful—who live on the river in a house composed of "rooms in which life was gathered, rooms in the morning sunlight, the floors spread with Oriental rugs . . . apricot, rouge and tan, rugs which though worn seemed to drink the sun, to collect its warmth; books, potpourris, cushion in colors of Matisse, objects glistening like evidence . . . clear crystal dice, pieces of staghorn, amber beads, boxes, sculptures." Yet the inner life of the couple is "mysterious . . . From far off it seems a unity . . . but closer it begins to separate, to break into light and shadow . . . Within there is no form, only prodigious detail that reaches everywhere: exotic sounds, spills of sunlight, foliage, fallen trees, small beasts that flee at the sound of a twig-snap, insects, silence, flowers."

Reading these words in 1975 one might have thought that *Light Years* was going to break one's heart the way *Tender Is the Night* did, or *Revolutionary Road*. In 2013, it might feel otherwise.

The novel that put Salter's name on the literary map was *A Sport and a Pastime*, published in 1967. The narrator is an American in his thirties, living in a provincial town in France, who is visited by a college dropout ten years his junior. This boy-man meets a girl in the town and, with her, falls into an extraordinary affair of sexual obsession. The book is a tour de force of erotic realism—no reader can help feeling weakened, then drained by the enveloping force of its nonstop sensuality. Again and again—and again!— we are given, through the astonishingly voyeuristic narrator mourning the approaching loss of his own virility, the same graphic description of the hypnotic sex that is the novel's reason for being. The boy's prick enters the girl every which way: it slides, it thrusts, it wedges, it jams, "it sinks like an iron bar into water"—and he comes and comes and comes. This is definitely the man's story. The girl slithers and grinds and moans but she is clearly instrumental: we never see her achieving orgasm, because her face is continually in the pillows. She is only and always taken from behind (about which more later.)

On occasion the narrator takes the train to Paris, and there he socializes. The description of a single party says it all. Given by a French journalist, a man who "has the calm irreverence one achieves only from close observation of the great," the party is attended by diplomats, writers, celebrities; an aging actress "made out of yesterdays," a man whose wife is a Whitney. The narrator tells us in a voice laced with knowing envy that "one meets a certain kind of people here . . . people with money and taste." The perfect complement to heroic sex.

A Sport and a Pastime achieved enormous critical success and a cult following that is still going strong: readers everywhere for whom the situation remains compelling, the sensuality transcendent, the prose riddled through with an essence of longing that achieves metaphor. Good enough. What is not good enough is that as the books and the years have accumulated the unwavering reverence in Salter's work for sex, money, and taste repeatedly delivers itself in the same lush style, but without any appreciable development. Which brings us to *All That Is,* a remarkable concentrate of the books that preceded it.

Philip Bowman is a World War II veteran. The battles, the comradeships, the shared dangers remain the emotional highlight of his life. After the war, he manipulates his way into Harvard, makes a few social connections, wanders around for a while and finally comes to rest in a small, classy New York publishing house, where he works as an editor for the next thirty years. He also has one affair after another. He does marry Vivian of Virginia horse-country wealth; but after the divorce, there is Enid and Christine and Anet and Ann. Women are at the very heart of things. Not women as fellow creatures but women as the source of an enraptured virility that alone makes life worth living for Bowman. Around the affairs collect the signature Salter preoccupation with wartime glory, money, and class distinction, and sex, sex, sex. Times without number in this book we are treated to an evocation of beautiful houses, elegant clothing, glamorous gatherings; and times without number "he parted her legs and knelt between them . . . caressed her for a long time . . . turned her over and put his hand on her shoulders and then slowly down along her body as it were the neck of a goose . . . He wanted it to last a long time . . . Ah, ah, ah. The walls were falling away. The city was collapsing like stars."

There isn't a woman in the book whom Bowman doesn't turn over and take from behind; by the same token, there isn't a woman in the book, except for the last one (and the returns aren't in on her), who doesn't leave him. Why this is we can never actually know, as we experience these characters—Bowman *and* the women—only through an accumulation of surfaces; we're never inside any of them. The self-knowledge required for reflection or interpretation is absent. Engagement with work or ideas or the world beyond the sensual self—elements that might prove revelatory—is nonexistent.

Ten pages from the end, an unknowing but somewhat fatigued Bowman, now in his late fifties, stands musing out the window at an office Christmas party. "He was under the spell of other Christmases. He was remembering the winter during the war, at sea, far from home and on the ship, Armed Forces Radio playing carols, 'Silent Night,' and everyone thinking back. With its deep nostalgia and hopeless longing it had been the most romantic Christmas of his life."

At this moment, the last love—another editor in the publishing house—makes her entrance. Bowman worries that it might be too late for him; in shorts his legs seem to belong to an old man. But then he puts on his Tripler & Co. suit (the midnight blue with a thin pinstripe) and feels reassured. Some months into the affair, the woman says she'd love to go to Venice. Bowman hesitates—he's been there so many times!—but he gradually relents. His weariness lifts, and he begins planning. Best to go in the fall, he tells her. "Yes," he says in the final line of the book. "Let's go in November. We'll have a great time."

Certainly, it is true that most writers have only one story in them—that is, as Flannery O'Connor put it, only one they can make come alive. Then again, it is also true that it is the writer's obligation to make the story tell more the third or fourth time around than it did the first. For this reviewer, Slater's work fails on that score. In his eighties he tells the story almost exactly as he told it in his forties.

The problem is that he should have been born ten or fifteen years earlier than 1925. Then the romantic realism of self-mythologizing postwar literature—the kind that rose with Hemingway after the First World War and sank with Irwin Shaw after the Second—might have allowed Salter to go on writing sentences like "In the riches of [her] smile one would never be lonely or forgotten" without penalty through a long writing life. Today, however, it is sad and confusing to read such sentences—so out of touch with the life we are actually living—emerging from the work of an artist whose love of expressive language is as much to be admired now as it was half a century ago.

8

Edna St. Vincent Millay

In 1970 Nancy Milford published a famous biography of Zelda Fitzgerald, one of the fabled bad girls of American literary bohemia. The book is remarkable for the power with which it brings to life the romantic disorder that plagued the Fitzgeralds—how *loved* they were for it! —and also for revealing how much more trapped in it was Zelda than Scott. While he could make literature out of their shared circumstance she, his raw material, could only be consumed by it. She had been adored for the chaos within: it was her gift and her karma. There was nothing for it but to go on being outrageous to the truly bitter end.

At the very same time that Zelda was riding the crest of her extraordinary wave, another famous bad girl of American arts was riding hers. This one, however, is known to us not as the companion to the talent but the talent itself. Madly bohemian, Edna St. Vincent Millay, in her glory years, was as well known for her capacity to arouse the national fantasy about free love and reckless living as for her poetry. She was, as Nancy Milford tells us, "the first American figure to rival the personal adulation of Byron." Millay, in fact, drew the same kind of crowds that Byron drew: "Her performing self made people feel they had seen the muse alive and just within reach . . . [S]he not only brought them to their feet, she brought them to her. In the heart of the Depression her collection of sonnets *Fatal Interview* sold 35,000 copies within the first two weeks of its publication." This wasn't because America had become a nation of poetry lovers.

Edna Millay was born in 1892 and grew up, in hardship and in beauty, on the coast of Maine. She was one of three daughters born to a poor, independent-minded mother (a wig-maker and visiting nurse) who, in 1900, told an incapable husband to get out, and set about raising her daughters alone. Cora Millay was an original: tough, smart, literate. Inside her rough edges a romantic was burning with odd ambition for her girls if not for herself: "I had a chip on my shoulder for them. It is a vicarious thing to live on the edge of everything, but with the parent against the world it is stronger yet . . . [T]hey always had a line out to the beautiful and the tragic . . . I let the girls realize their poverty: I let them realize what every advantage cost me in the effort to live."

They adored her inordinately—in her company, the ardor not for life but *of* life became a formative experience—and within the psyche of each girl this adoration for the mother wove itself into an unusual family romance. In the

'20s, in Greenwich Village, people watched Cora Millay and her three daughters rambling about together, raptly involved with one another, a little band of countrywomen hitting the big city, looking like some eerie version of *Little Women*. Inside the originality and high spirits something secret, mocking, untouchable: they were for one another as they would be for no one else; a prefiguration of all the loneliness to come.

Of course, at the beating-heart center was Edna—always Edna. They were there because of Edna; because Edna had written a famous poem ("Renascence") at twenty, received the support of a rich patron, gone to Vassar and then, in the spring of 1917, come to New York to begin her amazing career of poetry and seduction. As Malcolm Cowley remembered it, "They were each lovely girls. But Edna . . . [s]he'd break your heart. There was something wild and elusive about her."

She'd been that at twelve, she'd be that at forty: wild and elusive. Or, rather, intent on making people experience her as wild and elusive. This was the thing, always, at the heart of her character and of her work: her bold need for self-dramatization. Edmund Wilson put it best, and for countless others, when he described meeting her—again in the Village, in the '20s—at a party where she was reading her poems. Her voice, he said, was absolutely thrilling. It gave her the "power of imposing herself on others through a medium that unburdened the emotions of solitude. The company hushed and listened as people do to music—her authority was always complete . . . She was one of those women whose features are not perfect and who in their moments of dimness may not seem even pretty, but who, excited by the blood or the spirit, become almost supernaturally beautiful."

Dorothy Thompson—who knew Millay in Budapest, at the height of her fame, on a trip to Europe—put it another way: "She was a little bitch, a genius, a cross between a gamin and an angel . . . She sat before the glass and combed her lovely hair, over and over. Narcissan. She really never loved anyone except herself . . . I had to go back to Vienna and left her the toast of half the town. Handed her all I had because she was an angel . . . She might have left Josef [Thompson's husband] alone, but not that, either "

It had nothing to do with sensuality, everything to do with the romantic exercise of will: a will bent on inducing lifelong yearning in those around her. The magnetism lay in a triumph of attitude that had been hers since girlhood. She saw herself as linked to a higher destiny. In the poems she would often, with spice and daring, pronounce those she seduced ennobled because they had been loved and left by *her*. They should all, she felt, be proud to have served the higher cause—the sheer intensity—of her self-devotion.

Nothing and no one mattered except the intensity. How to keep it alive became the central question of her life. The answer, of course, was always the same: to drink, sleep around, and make art—nonstop. Before she was through, there'd been a thousand men in her bed, a few thousand drinks under her belt, and more money made from the writing of poetry than any other American poet had seen before or, perhaps, since. The fame came because her need to be herself at all costs meshed perfectly with the need of the time. In a profile of her in the *New Yorker* in 1925, the writer explains why hers is the voice of the moment: "[T]he poems celebrate the loves of [the] footloose . . . The only genuine surrender is to death . . . It is the only intensity available after a love that has burned on nothing but itself"; the writer goes on to observe that the generation that had just gone to war "had seen nothing so accurate about itself in print."

This poet, once so beloved, is entirely unknown today. We do not read her work or, if we do, we experience very little of what was experienced during her lifetime. If you ask why this is so, the answer will probably be, "They're senti-mental." By which is meant, not that Millay's formality or subject matter or attitudes are out of fashion but, rather, that the poems simply do not go deep enough. The material is not sufficiently transformed. If it was, it will be said, none of the rest would matter. The poems would then be news that stayed news.

Yet, as a figure, Edna Millay compels. Something in her life signifies. It occurred to me, reading Milford's biogra-phy, that she was, not the Byron of her day but, more accurately, the Anne Sexton of her day. Another amazing seducer-through-poetry whose public readings drove people wild but whose work now—alone on the page, thirty years later, without the special pleading of a live performance— has much less impact than it did when the collective reader could feel, behind the words, the stirring presence of the actor-poet. In the flesh, these two literary vamps both generated a powerful allure—to which they themselves became addicted—that spread the reputation of the poems far and wide. As a result, they hungered to remain vamps forever and, in fact, never progressed, either of them, in the life or in the work, beyond this urgency. In each case the vamping can now be seen as a harbinger of some internal nihilism, something determined to eat itself alive that seems emblematic of the time—and it is this that holds our attention.

These women were possessed of a blazing, raging, murderous extremity: brilliant, driven, unforgiving. Compelled to consume all that came its way, inevitably it consumed itself. Sylvia Plath might be added to their number—certainly she died for the rage not the poetry—and, of course, there was Zelda Fitzgerald. The disparities in literary talent among them notwithstanding, they are all vivid examples of a kind of willed temperamental outrage at having been born into ordinary human damage. They be damned if they'd submit—and they were.

Trapped in the lives of these rather fabulous creatures is a piece of glory and sorrow on the grand scale. The social and sexual anarchy to which both Millay and Fitzgerald were seriously devoted is of a kind that no experience can influence. Hard, mean, and immutable, it inflicts an intolerable loneliness, and indeed, the loneliness cannot be tolerated. Sexton and Plath killed themselves and Zelda Fitzgerald went mad; Millay, on the other hand, perhaps the most complicated of the lot, devised an ending for herself altogether more interesting. In the last part of her life, she lived alone, with her revering husband, in a rural retreat called Steepletop. Here, a lovely estate three hours from New York City was created solely to serve Edna's art. But as time went on, and the power of her youthful beauty evaporated, it was her melancholy not her art that was served. She retreated steadily into booze and drugs. Her husband, insistent upon the genius in his keeping, continued to keep the house in perpetual readiness for Edna's muse. As they waited, the place grew shabbier and shabbier. She fell into morphine addiction, so did he, less and less did they leave home, and at last they were both buried alive in what had become an eerie fantasy of the life they were waiting to live. In short: Steepletop became Sunset Boulevard.

9

The Reading Group

There are five of us. We've been reading memoir together for ten years. We meet only when all of us can make it. Some years, that means only six or seven times. Even so, these meetings often seem to come at the kind of inconvenient moment that lives like ours—the ones eaten up with scheduling—are forever manufacturing. Yet no one wants to give up the group.

It's not the reading itself that holds us together—how many hours have we each sat, eyelids propped open against the unexpected dullness of a famously great book. I don't think it's even the conversation that the book gives rise to. It is, rather, the atmosphere that we occupy while we are meeting that each of us has grown reluctant to do without.

I used to think it was the conversation. Not that the exchange is necessarily one of depth, or originality, or even agreement. To the contrary, disagreement among us, strong and well-argued, is routine; it is, in fact, what we look forward to. Among us, disagreement is a stimulant not a depressant: the opposing view against which your own defense gives you back more of yourself than you had before. Argument in the group leaves us, as George Meredith said good conversation should leave you, feeling refreshed by the opportunity to experience social intercourse as an act of self-expansion.

Really, it's quite remarkable, this ever-recurring demonstration of a thing we all know about—the dynamics of good talk—but only rarely encounter. What is especially remarkable about the group is that it is only *as* a group that we achieve the shared temperament necessary for such conversation. We have all known each other for twenty years and more, in one context or another, and while each of us values the others in the abstract, outside of the group none of us meet by design. One on one, we are a great example of the near-miss so common among sufficiently like-minded people who should blossom in each other's company but do not. Over the years, each of us has talked books with one of the others, only to emerge from an exchange that all too quickly reaches closure, leaving one or both feeling puzzled or chagrined, even melancholy. But when we come together as a group, some vital commonality in the way we *all* read intervenes to reduce the irritation and discomfort that, one on one, we inevitably inflict on one another.

That very first evening—we were reading Rousseau, I remember—I found Leonard's remarks dipped in that customary acid negativism of his that always puts me on the overheated defensive. As he spoke I found my own as yet unformulated remarks beginning to shrivel in my head. But Claire laughed warmly, and delivered an opinion so intellectually soothing that it made Myra clever, and the discussion took off. When my turn came I had gained the distance necessary to register the merit of a point Leonard had made earlier, and was able to speak amiably to that alone. All evening I watched as this kind of serendipity occurred repeatedly among us, each and every time creating a tone sufficiently free of tension that the conversation knew no closure.

It is this tone that has made us mesh as a group; again and again, it helps shape sentences that set each of our thoughts free, makes them fly out unguarded, secure in the knowledge that even if challenged they will be received. That meshing not only opens us to our own thought, it obligates us to responsiveness. Obligation has made each of us, in our opening presentations, dig deeper. Inevitably, digging deeper gives someone the chance to hit pay dirt. Many is the night that one or more of us has walked in, thinking, "I don't have one damned thing to say about this book," and has ended by delivering one of the more memorable insights of the evening because another of us has connected so strongly with the book in hand that the atmosphere is galvanized; then all are released from the inertness of mind that an absence of engagement imposes. Who connects with what book is always a revelation. We once read George Kennan's memoir, and this is how the session began:

"A civilized and poetic being," said Daniel.

"Weak passions, strong ambitions, and a continual sense of himself in the world," said I.

"A cold warrior riddled with nostalgia," said Myra.

"The Russians are his demonized childhood," said Claire.

"This is the man who has humiliated me my entire life," said Leonard.

It was Leonard to whom the book belonged that night. His dislike of Kennan—powerful yet tempered—had touched a useful nerve. Leonard is a sixty-year-old gay man, and for him, middle-class liberalism has always been the enemy. When he spoke it was out of strong emotion informed by years of reflection anchored in a crucial piece of identity. His critique opened an unexpected vein in the conversation. None of us had ever before considered Kennan in the light of Leonard's take; and none of us would ever again see the courtly diplomat as we had before. The evening was a high.

Every book has its poetic respondent among us, the one for whom the book, whatever its shortcomings or eccentricities, delivers an inner clarity that resonates in that part of the expressive self where intelligence serves sensibility. The surprise, as I say, is always supplied by who resonates to whom. (Canetti? Augustine? *You?* Oscar *Wilde,* for God's sake!)   No one was more surprised than me to find myself stirred on one occasion by Thomas de Quincey, on another by Loren Eiseley—an English drug addict and a Midwestern depressive, both of them men formed in times and places deeply foreign to my own. Yet in each of this unlikely pair I saw a self-created loneliness—neurotic, stubborn, overriding—that was central to the life. I knew that one down to the ground. These memoirs made me know better something that I already knew (exactly what had happened between Leonard and Kennan). In their presence *I* clarified.

It is the reading group that has made me realize how very closely the relation we have to books resembles the one we have with people. Myra is one of the smartest readers in the group—and one of the narrowest. It matters not how intimidating the reputation of a book might be, or how well established its author, she is relentless in her resistance to nostalgia or sentimentality, which she perceives as self-deception. "He doesn't know himself," is her favorite opening sentence. Yet quite often, there came a book that would receive from her the dispensation we inexplicably extend to those who arouse in us the mystery of temperamental connection.

Daniel and I had both read biographies of H. G. Wells that significantly contradicted, even belied his own account of his life. Our discussion of these discrepancies the night we read Wells's memoir, *Experiment in Autobiography*, was turning the session into an amused seminar on "truth" in a personal narrative. When Myra's turn came she amazed us all by stating flatly that it mattered not at all that Wells had white-washed his own story. It mattered only that in this memoir we had a profoundly satisfying evocation of an atmosphere of *mind*; this Wells had delivered, so brilliantly and so fully, that it made her yearn for a time when an excellent intelligence could live out a long life informed by an undiminished belief in the inevitable progress of science and socialism.

None of us had ever heard Myra put down her red pencil and recklessly—hedonistically—embrace a book. As she talked, we could see that it was nothing in particular in the Wells memoir that had enraptured her, it wasn't even Wells himself. It was, in some remarkable way, a wholeness of being in the book that had touched the place in her where *she* felt whole. Exactly what we experience in friendship or in love: the connection that returns us to our own expressiveness. As we listened to Myra, everyone in the room seemed to draw a deeper breath. The air brightened visibly. I was reminded of something Randall Jarrell had once written: that it was an atmosphere of reading that we wished to inhabit, one where reading is as elemental as air and light and water.

I think often of Jarrell when the group meets. How real and close to the heart he seems when I am most moved by this live thing that occurs, almost every time, between a book and its one true reader, and by the extraordinary fallout this vividness gives rise to among the rest of us. It is then that I understand most intensely how devoted humanity is to the act of making literature because it leads to the act of reading.

CULTURE

10

Uncle Tom's Cabin

It is now a century and a half since *Uncle Tom's Cabin* was published in the spring of 1852. Within a year of publication the book had sold 305,000 copies in the United States, and something like 2.5 million all over the world. Its impact, among English speakers especially, was phenomenal. Lord Palmerston read it three times and called it statesman-like. Abraham Lincoln, when he met Harriet Stowe, remarked famously, "So this is the little lady who made this big war." After the war, however, sales declined rapidly, and by the 1890s, the book was out of print, where it remained for fifty years.

But *Uncle Tom's Cabin* was destined for the kind of mythic fame that would have made its author drop her jaw and shade her eyes. The characters were kept alive by successive stage dramatizations that exploited them for their comic and melodramatic elements, each one moving ever farther from the original until finally the famous novel was transformed into a vaudeville that, by the 1920s, compelled the writers of the Harlem Renaissance to blast it to kingdom come with their hot scorn of "Tom-ism." Thus, as Edmund Wilson observed in *Patriotic Gore*, his great study of Civil War literature, "To expose oneself in maturity to *Uncle Tom* may prove a startling experience." Indeed.

I read the book recently for the first time, not only to discover that there are no dogs snapping at Eliza's heels as she crosses the ice, that Simon Legree is not an overseer, that Topsy bears a strong resemblance to the sinister love child in *The Scarlet Letter*, and that Tom is a Christ figure, but also to discover the real shocker: the unexpectedness of Stowe's intelligence, the depth and the breadth of it. A masterpiece of American literature had lived inside me since childhood as the sum of those distortions that popular culture and civil rights rhetoric had imposed on it for most of its lifetime. If ever a book proved that politics and literature are inextricably bound, *Uncle Tom's Cabin* is it.

What Lord Palmerston meant when he called the book statesmanlike is that Stowe creates a slowly unfolding, steadily more encompassing picture of how slavery was actually lived out in the United States among slaves, slave owners and traders, bounty hunters, and Christian do-gooders (both genuine and hypocritical). It is a picture drawn with sufficient analytic and descriptive power to make every creature on the landscape a felt reality.

The structure of the book is simple. Tom, a slave on a Kentucky estate, is bought and sold twice, and Eliza, a slave on the same estate, becomes a runaway. These twin events provide the two major strands of storytelling that the book develops. Eliza's fate is resolved successfully when she falls into the hands of Quakers on the Underground Railroad who transport her (along with her child and recovered husband) to Canada. Tom's journey is of an altogether other nature. Each of Tom's successive owners forces him farther south—farther into hell—on a Pilgrim's Progress that is meant to account for much of the world of slave masters. To begin with, there is the weak, kindly philistine, Arthur Shelby of Kentucky, then the poetic, spiritually inert Augustine St. Clare of New Orleans and, at last, the pathologically self-hating Simon Legree hidden away in rural Louisiana. Holding the drama together is Tom's steady progress toward his own Christ-like death; a death, that is, of course, a foregone conclusion.

Metaphysical schemes aside, the characters in *Uncle Tom's Cabin* are remarkably absorbing. In the first household we meet Tom and Eliza, Tom's wife, Chloe, and the Shelbys' liberal son, George; in the second, St. Clare and his daughter, Little Eva, the wild-child slave, Topsy, and St. Clare's self-consciously Christian cousin from the north, Ophelia; in Simon Legree's house of horrors, it is Eliza's long-lost mother, the magnificent Cassy (another character Hawthorne could have written) who compels attention. These people all take their places in the allegory, and the force and clarity with which each one comes alive on the page, emerging from a prose that is essentially without art, is amazing.

Stowe was a writer with a mission. Her mission was to make mid–nineteenth-century America see that it had betrayed itself with slavery, and her excellent mind told her to work hard to create characters who would move, as well as instruct, readers. So we see the vanity of Arthur Shelby's weakness, feel the anxiety behind Simon Legree's murderousness, and are shocked by the mad integrity of Topsy's wildness as well as the terrible limitation of Ophelia's knee-jerk Christianity.

Tom is the figure in whom reposes Stowe's idea of genuine Christianity—the man who cannot close his heart or raise his hand against another, even at the risk of losing his life—and Tom is also the repository of typically radical fantasies about the Other. On arriving at St. Clare's beautiful house in New Orleans,

> Tom got down from the carriage, and looked about with an air of calm, still enjoyment. The negro, it must be remembered, is an exotic of one of the most gorgeous and superb countries in the world, and he has, deep in his heart, a passion for all that is splendid, rich, and fanciful . . . If ever Africa shall show an elevated and cultivated race—and come it must, some time, her turn to figure in the great drama of human improvement—life will awake there a gorgeousness and splendor of which our cold western tribes faintly have conceived. In that far-off mystic land . . . will awake new forms of art, new styles of splendor; and the negro race, no longer despised and trodden down, will, perhaps, show forth some of the latest and most magnificent revelations of human life . . .

Little Eva is Tom's saintly counterpart. When everyone is terrorized by Topsy's suicidal unruliness, Eva alone tames the wretched black girl by smoothing her face with a kindly hand. It is often Eva who is the catalyst for plain thinking in the central section of the book. In one crucial scene, St. Clare and Ophelia sit on a veranda watching the little girl climb up onto Tom's lap. Ophelia, the complicated do-gooder, finds herself viscerally disgusted at the sight of the white child hugging the black man, and St. Clare observes,

> You would think no harm in a child's caressing a large dog, even if he was black; but a creature that can think, and reason, and feel, and is immortal, you shudder at . . . I know the feeling among some of you northerners . . . You loathe them as you would a snake or a toad, yet you are indignant at their wrongs. You would not have them abused; but you don't want to have anything to do with them yourselves. You would send them to Africa, out of your sight and smell, and then send a missionary . . . to elevate them . . .

Gazing at Eva and Tom, St. Clare murmurs, "What would the poor and lowly do, without children? . . . Your little child is your only true democrat . . ."

Ophelia is amazed and chastened by these thoughts, and thinks him on the verge of becoming an abolitionist, whereupon, he instantly punctures his own balloon. "Nothing," he assures her, "is easier than talking," and recalls, appropriately enough, that "Shakespeare makes somebody say, 'I could sooner show twenty what were good to be done, than be one of the twenty to follow my own showing.'"

Culture

At the unforgettable heart of the novel stands St. Clare. It is through him that Stowe makes the largest sense of things. In the middle of the novel he delivers a fifteen-page disquisition worthy of George Eliot on the existential meaning of slavery. The speech is both profound and shocking. He is the Ashley Wilkes of *Uncle Tom's Cabin*: a developed sensibility rendered useless by an immobilized will. His words, his destiny, his very being come to haunt the reader. In his person the hope of civilization is both aroused and deflated. Through him we feel acutely the limited use of an educated intelligence as opposed to that of a clarified spirit moved to urgency.

St. Clare is the good German under the Nazis, or the nerveless Tolstoyan shrugging off serfdom, or the liberal white South African living with apartheid. St. Clare is any one of us, at any time in history. In 1858, in a collection of articles, letters, and slave auction notices called "A Key to Uncle Tom's Cabin," Stowe published a letter written in 1773 by Patrick Henry in which Henry says of slavery, "[T]hat this abominable practice has been introduced . . . at a time when the rights of humanity are defined and understood with precision, in a country above all others fond of liberty . . . is as repugnant to humanity as it is inconsistent . . . Would anyone believe that I am master of slaves of my own purchase? I am drawn along by the general inconvenience of living here without them. I will not, I cannot, justify it."

We see why it took Moses forty years to lead the Jews out of the desert. How dominating is appetite, how enveloping immediate experience! Even the philosophically minded among us capitulate, ultimately, to the narrowest sense of personal need. Political time moves at a snail's pace because it is only with nearly insurmountable difficulty that moral discomfort takes root in the best of people, forcing an imperative out of a complaint; so viscerally repugnant is it for a critical mass to find the prevailing system unbearable, much less prepare to take up arms against it. Impossible, then, for one and all, victims and victimizers alike, to do more than rage or regret, suffer or run, pursue or die. Harriet Stowe was a fervent Christian, but she might just as easily have been a theoretical revolutionary, such is the cast of her mind.

Uncle Tom's Cabin has the power to make any reader remember that if arms are not taken up during a time in which some human beings are perceived and treated as less than human, then everyone alive will have much to answer for. It is impossible to read the book and not find yourself thinking, "If the time was now, and the place was here where would I be standing on this landscape of human insufficiency"?

11

Rachel Carson

In 1858, the Victorian poet and critic Edmund Gosse was a nine-year-old child. That spring and summer, he and his father spent their days collecting marine specimens in the tidal pools gathered on the Cornwall seashore. Of this time and place, Gosse later wrote:

> [T]he rocks between tide and tide were submarine gardens of a beauty that seemed often to be fabulous and was positively delusive, since if we delicately lifted the weed-curtains of a windless pool, though we might for a moment see its sides and floor paved with living blossoms, ivory-white, rosy-red, orange and amethyst, yet all that panoply would melt away, furled into the hollow rock if we so much as dropped a pebble in to disturb the magic dream . . .
>
> All this is long over, and done with. The ring of living beauty drawn about our shores was a very thin and

fragile one. It had existed all those centuries solely in consequence of the indifference, the blissful ignorance of man. These rock-basins . . . filled with still water almost as pellucid as the upper air itself, thronged with beautiful sensitive forms of life—they exist no longer. An army of "collectors" has passed over them, and ravaged every corner of them. The fairy paradise has been violated, the exquisite product of centuries of natural selection has been crushed . . . No one will see again on the shores of England what I saw in my early childhood.

These words were written in 1907. Half a century later Rachel Carson, the American marine biologist and nature writer, was saying much the same thing about the even further desecration of nature, for which she, too, held humanity (in the twentieth century, more than in any other) responsible. Now, another half century on, we read the fiftieth-anniversary edition of *Silent Spring*, Carson's great brief for nature's prosecution of the human species, and are sobered anew. Thinking about what has and has not been done in recognition of her plea that human beings realize that all species on earth are dependent on one another to preserve the environment in which they will either live or perish together, it still seems to me that our fate will be the latter.

What Carson saw in the late 1950s was that on a planet threatened by the reckless use of pesticides, and equally imperiled by the radioactive fallout from recurrent nuclear bomb tests, the natural world was literally under siege—and we along with it. As William Souder, her latest biographer, tells us, Carson intuited that "pesticides and radiation [were] capable of damaging the genetic material that guides the machinery of living cells and provides the blueprint for each succeeding generation." These were "the inevitable and potentially lethal developments of the modern age, each one a consequence, as she put it bluntly in *Silent Spring*, of 'the impetuous and heedless pace of man rather than the deliberate pace of nature.'"

A dramatic world debate erupted upon the publication of *Silent Spring* in 1962, with many in government and industry shaking a collective fist at Carson, the melodramatic alarmist, and many more among the press and the general public lionizing Carson, the selfless whistle-blower. From that day to this, her name arouses anger and frustration alike among those who still oppose her insistence that we pull back severely on the use of pesticides—as well as those who insist, If we don't do as she says, the earth is doomed. Whatever one's position, there is no denying that *Silent Spring* has become—and will remain—one of the most influential books of the twentieth century.

Rachel Carson was born in May of 1907 in Springdale, Pennsylvania, a small hardscrabble town fourteen miles from Pittsburgh, into a genteel family that had fallen on permanent hard times. Although there was a Mr. Carson, Rachel's true "parents" were her adoring mother (an impassioned nature lover) and the woods and fields around the Carson homestead, which mother taught daughter to commune with. For the young Rachel, mother and nature became inextricably bound together and, as it turned out, she never had to pull the dyad apart: throughout her life she communed with nature and she lived with her mother.

By the time she entered nearby Pennsylvania College for Women, Carson was more than ready to fall under the spell of a dynamic science teacher who, as Souder tells us, taught that "all life was interconnected, and seen in the light of evolution this means, as Carson came to realize, that every day in the world offered evidence of all the years of the world that had come before." For the young Rachel this insight was magical, as it still is for every budding scientist: it became the romantic touchstone of her life, never to be replaced by another.

Upon graduation from college, she applied for and was given a scholarship to study zoology at Johns Hopkins; but the summer before she entered graduate school she received a fellowship at the Marine Biological Laboratory at Woods Hole, Massachusetts, and here she discovered something vital about herself: she was no good at hands-on science. What she was good at was doing research in the library— and writing imaginatively about her findings. This, she quickly saw, she could do well and happily for the rest of her life. The library and the typewriter together told her who she was: a writer with a talent for making science come alive on the page.

In 1935, she went to work for the federal government, writing radio scripts for the Bureau of Fisheries. Within six months of her arrival at the bureau, her boss asked her to write something "of a general sort" about the sea. The result was an essay so engaging that her intelligent boss said it was too good for a minor government publication and suggested that she submit it to the *Atlantic Monthly,* where it was immediately accepted and published under the title "Undersea." As Souder explains:

> The essay was an animated distillation of seemingly everything that Carson knew firsthand or had learned from the scientific literature about the life that crowded the sea, from the water's edge to the high-tide mark to the depths of black chasms beneath the open ocean. It went beyond mere description of the lives of starfish and eels and crabs and fish into the deeper meanings of oceanic natural history. Here, in the tidal wash and beneath the waves appeared nature's demonstration of the systemic biological forces that link all life in the present and through the ages—the myriad churning, interrelated existences that are the leading edge of evolutionary history.

It was the seed from which Carson's first three books grew, all published between 1941 and 1955: *Under the Sea-Wind, The Sea Around Us* (this one made her internationally famous), and *The Edge of the Sea.* These were the books that demonstrated her writerly grasp of what many others had also seen, but could not make dramatic. Or put another way: she was always part of a web of people whose interests matched her own. There were marine biologists, professional and amateur, doing the same thing at the same time all over the world; that's how she was able to consult so many experts over the years. But the element missing from their work was, as Souder writes, "the voice of someone standing above this elemental environment and feeling within it the slow pulse of geologic time and the mighty force of evolution that lies inside and behind the surging waters—a voice that belonged more naturally to Rachel Carson."

It was, however, to be a good ten years between the writing of that original piece in 1936 and the conscious recognition that the sea, where all life began, was to become her all-in-all. In spring 1946 Carson was asked to write a series of pamphlets describing the federal wildlife refuges and explaining the work that the bureau (now renamed the U.S. Fish and Wildlife Service) was doing in them. The project was called Conservation in Action, and out of it came her mature awareness that all earthly species are dependent on an inextricable web of interactions that connects every living thing, one to another. Thus, Carson the conservationist evolved into Carson the ecologist.

The first subject of these 1946 pamphlets was Plum Island, Massachusetts. It was here that she began seriously to fall in love with the ocean in general, and the New England seafronts in particular. "Standing at the water's edge," Souder tells us, "the loneliness of the Atlantic was palpable." To Carson, that loneliness spoke volumes.

In 1952 she bought a piece of land on a rocky promontory on Southport Island near Boothbay Harbor, Maine, and built a house to which she traveled every summer from her home in the Washington suburb of Silver Spring, Maryland. Here, for the remainder of her comparatively short life she watched, studied, brooded over, and exulted in the ocean beneath her window, bending over its tidal pools, gathering the marine life swarming in them, walking out on the rocks early and late, and all the while keeping copious notes and records of the daily and seasonal changes of the ocean itself.

On Southport Island Carson met Dorothy Freeman who, along with her husband, Stanley, was her nearest neighbor. The Freemans were an amiable couple who also revered nature, and very quickly the three became good friends. In time, the two women fell in love. Dorothy remained contentedly married to Stanley (neither she nor Rachel wanted it any other way), but the women spent large amounts of time together on Southport Island in the summer and, whenever possible, they met secretly through-out the year in Washington, Boston, or New York—to cuddle and commune, I think (though who can ever know?), not to actually make love.

Upon the publication in 1995 of a volume of the many letters Carson and Freeman wrote to each other, Carson was claimed by gays as one of their own. I, however, cannot imagine the virginal Rachel an active lesbian; in fact, it's almost impossible to imagine her in a state of carnal desire at all. I would say rather that once in her life she fell in love with a person, and when she did the object of her love happened to be a woman. Carson was one of those people, oddly made, whose sublimation of the normal passions—in her case, through nature—was absolute. The letters she wrote to Dorothy Freeman are intensely romantic, but they are not at all sexual.

Nonetheless, the attachment was powerful, and im-mensely important to both women, enriching their lives for the eleven years it endured, ending only with Carson's death in 1964. A miserable irony here is that while she was writing about the dying earth, she herself was dying. By the time *Silent Spring* was published, two years had passed since Carson had been diagnosed with a breast cancer that kept on metastasizing. She was fifty-two and had four nightmarishly painful years to live—and, American stoic that she was, she refused to let a day of them be lost to self-pity. In February 1963, more dead than alive, she wrote to Freeman: "The main thing I want to say, dear, is that we are not going to get bogged down in unhappiness about all this. We are going to be happy, and go on enjoying all the lovely things that give life meaning—sunrise and sunset, moonlight on the bay, music and good books, the song of thrushes and the wild cries of geese passing over."

And she kept on working. She continued to travel extensively on behalf of her sobering but beautiful book—speaking, lecturing, testifying in Washington, and starring in a television documentary built around the book's argument. Everyone around her, including Eric Sevareid, the program's distinguished interviewer, feared she would not live to see it aired. But she did. *CBS Reports: The Silent Spring of Rachel Carson*—now considered a milestone in the history of television reporting—was viewed by millions of Americans on April 3, 1963. Almost exactly one year later, on April 14, 1964, Carson died.

A year after her death, a book called *The Sense of Wonder*—which had begun life in 1956 as an essay called "Help Your

Child to Wonder"—was released under Carson's name. In the year that she was dying, Carson undertook to revise (and rename) the piece, and have it illustrated by the dramatic photographs that she'd always wanted taken around her house in Maine. But time ran out on her, and the essay was republished in 1965 pretty much as it had been a decade earlier. Thirty years later, a photographer named Nick Kelsh found an old copy of *The Sense of Wonder* and took the photographs he thought Carson would have wanted to complete the book. In 1998, the essay was published again, now accompanied by Kelsh's dramatic images of woods, clouds, and ocean, thereby fulfilling magnificently Carson's yearning to see the quintessential statement of her life's work served well.

The essay begins with something close to a statement of purpose:

> One stormy autumn night when my nephew Roger was about twenty months old I wrapped him in a blanket and carried him down to the beach in the rainy darkness. Out there, just at the edge of where-we-couldn't-see, big waves were thundering in, dimly seen white shapes that boomed and shouted and threw great handfuls of froth at us. Together we laughed for pure joy—he a baby meeting for the first time the wild tumult of Oceanus, I with the salt of half a lifetime of sea love in me. But I think we felt the same spine-tingling response to the vast, roaring ocean and the wild night around us.

It goes on:

> It was hardly a conventional way to entertain one so young, I suppose, but now, with Roger a little past his fourth birthday, we are continuing that sharing of adventures in the world of nature that we began in his babyhood, and I think the results are good. The sharing includes nature in storm as well as calm, by night as well as day, and is based on having fun together.
>
> We have let Roger share our enjoyment of things people ordinarily deny children because they are inconvenient, interfering with bedtime, or involving wet clothing that has to be changed or mud that has to be cleaned off the rug ... I think we have felt that the memory of such a scene, photographed year after year by his child's mind, would mean more to him in manhood than the sleep he was losing.

The essay ends with her urging all parents to do for their children what she is doing for Roger because "if a child is to keep alive his inborn sense of wonder without any such gift from the fairies, he needs the companionship of at least one adult who can share it, rediscovering with him the joy, excitement and mystery of the world we live in." In my mind's eye I see Edmund Gosse nodding his head with the intensity of pleasure that connects one sympathetic sensibility to another.

12

Justice: What's the Right Thing to Do?

When I was young I thought that Hillel's "do unto others as you would have others do unto you"—the Golden Rule—was all the political theory necessary to make the world a good place in which to live. The Rule demanded only that I honor the same irreducible humanity in my fellows that I identified in myself. Just as I understood that I wished—no, *needed*—to not be dismissed, discounted, or traduced; restrained, cheated, or humiliated; robbed, raped, or murdered; so I understood that all other persons needed the same. This practice alone would provide the equality necessary to make all of us see ourselves in one another.

Equality. The word itself moved me, made my heart sing. Instinctively, I felt that equality was the key to human comradeship. In fact, I thought that it almost didn't matter how impoverishing or threatening a circumstance might be, so long as it was experienced equally. Repeatedly, throughout history, it had been shown that the most soul-destroying of conditions—wars, plagues, depressions—could be borne if shared equally. (A recent study, published in the United States as *The Spirit Level: Why Greater Equality Makes Societies Stronger*, actually argues that everything—life expectancy, infant mortality, obesity levels, crime rates, literacy scores, even garbage collection—improves in societies that are more rather than less equal). It was inequality, I was certain, that did the damage; inequality that destroyed one's innate sense of self-worth.

Not all political philosophers agree with me that equality is the word (that is, the concept) to concentrate on. For instance, Harvard professor Michael Sandel, absorbed by the question of how to make a good society, certainly thinks justice is the better word with which to address the ethical dilemmas that arise when we make decisions about "the right thing to do"—either on our own behalf, or on behalf of society.

Justice: What's the Right Thing to Do? is a book-length summary of a celebrated survey course on the moral basis of political philosophies ranging from Aristotle to John Rawls, given by Sandel, a remarkably skilled teacher who, over the course of some thirty years, has taught himself how to be undergraduate-lucid: anyone who has reached the age of reason can read the book. Its cleverness lies, especially, in Sandel's continual re-creation of homely situations that allow his readers to consult their feelings, while demanding that they use their reason in trying to figure out whether this or that approach to a question of justice makes sense. As Kathleen Sullivan, professor at Stanford Law School and a former teaching fellow of Sandel's, remembers it, "He posed moral dilemmas so acute one could escape the agony only by thinking."

Three approaches to justice—the welfare of the community at large, the rights of the individual, the value of good citizenship—are the heart of Sandel's matter. How to reason one's way through the thicket of argument both for and against each of these perspectives—all concerned with the relation between rights and obligations—is the subject of this book. In service to it, Sandel puts up, then knocks down, then resuscitates the reasoning of political philosophers who have struggled, over many centuries, to understand what it is that a human being needs in order to feel that he or she is being treated justly. Sandel posits an opinion about "the right thing to do," then reflects on that opinion, then works to name the principle on which it is based.

Roughly speaking, ancient theories of justice were concerned with the making of a morally responsible citizen, while modern theories are concerned with the freedom of the individual. None of these theories can separate cleanly out from one another—"Devoted as we are to freedom . . . the conviction that justice involves virtue as well as choice runs deep"—but, Sandel suggests, political philosophy, as a practice, can "give shape to the arguments we have, and bring moral clarity to the alternatives we confront as democratic citizens."

What subsequently comes under discussion are Aristotle's devotion to the virtue of citizenship; Jeremy Bentham's to utilitarianism (the greatest happiness for the greatest number); Robert Nozick's to libertarianism (my person and my goods are mine and mine alone to do with as I please); John Rawls's to an equalizing "fairness" that owes much to Immanuel Kant, the philosopher who struggled hardest with the question of the individual's rights and obligations in a modern society.

For Kant, Sandel tells us, "morality . . . is about respecting persons as ends in themselves." No social end is justified—whatever the gain or advantage—if its achievement depends on making instrumental use of other people, because such usage is degrading; to feel degraded is to know injustice. One must always treat humanity, Kant insisted, "whether in your own person or the person of any other," as an end-in-itself, never simply as a means, so as to avoid that degradation. This was one formulation of his "categorical imperative."

By declaring the definition of moral worth to be that which treats each and every person—including oneself—as objectively and unconditionally valuable, Kant requires not so much that people *ask* for justice as that they teach themselves how to *dispense* justice. Why? Because that, he said, is the road to freedom. For Kant, we are told, freedom was not about appetite and acquisition, it was about agency. To hold oneself responsible for one's own actions was to achieve agency.

Two centuries after Kant, the American political philosopher John Rawls took another shot at justice, society, and the individual. For Rawls, justice is fairness; his intellectual struggle was to lay out the argument for a society that could achieve it. Here is how he reasoned: No one is intrinsically more worthy or more deserving than anyone else of a favored starting place in society. If you are rewarded because you are blessed with wealth, beauty, or talent— endowed with drive, intelligence, or self-confidence—it is only because you are lucky enough to be living in a society that happens to value these qualities. The rules of the particular game into which you were born have determined the social agreement in your favor. But what of those not so favored? Are they to be inordinately punished while you are inordinately rewarded? A just society will be one that aims at eliminating those levels of disparity so huge they are experienced as what Kant would have called degrading. How do we approach the making of such a society?

Rawls's answer, Sandel tells us, is simple: basic liberties for all (such as freedom of speech, movement, religious belief), fair opportunities regardless of social class, and social and economic inequalities so manipulated that the *least* fortunate of a society's citizens rather than the most will be taken into consideration. Which means denying the free market the right to call the social shots. Those who are born lucky will not be held back, but luck will not permit a super privileged life to be lived side by side with a super deprived life. The gifted will be free to develop and exercise their talents—and no doubt, to the swift will go the race— but the social understanding is that, beyond an agreed-upon point, "the rewards these talents reap in the market belong to the community as a whole." Rawls's theory thus embraces the Kantian link between respect and self-respect: the expectation is that if the individual in society is accorded the means of insuring sufficient self-respect, the need to exert power over others will dissipate; and with that dissipation, moral (that is, social) responsibility will come as close to actuality as we can get.

"Whether or not [Rawls's] theory of justice ultimately succeeds," Sandel remarks generously, "it represents the most compelling case for a more equal society that American political philosophy has yet produced." I say generously because he disagrees strongly with Rawls's essential position that a "political conception of the person" as an individual is central to any workable idea of a just society. For Sandel, the claims of those "loyalties and attachments" that defy pure individual interests—family, religion, patriotism—are the very meaning of society.

At this point Sandel himself, as philosopher rather than as teacher, weighs in, pitching a communitarian view that argues, much as Aristotle argued, that "only by living in a polis . . . do we fully realize our nature as human beings." Egalitarian or libertarian theories of justice, that place a higher value on rights than on the communitarian good, Sandel declares,

> have a powerful appeal . . . Despite its appeal, however, this vision of freedom is flawed . . . If we understand ourselves as free and independent selves, unbound by moral ties we haven't chosen, we can't make sense of a range of moral and political obligations that we commonly recognize, even prize . . . obligations of solidarity and loyalty, historic memory and religious faith . . .

Sandel's course is exhilarating; more than exhilarating; exciting in its ability to persuade this student/reader, time and again, that the principle *now* being invoked—on this page, in this chapter—is the one to deliver the sufficiently inclusive guide to the making of a decent life. Yes, I found myself thinking, as one philosopher after another paraded his elegant thinking, this sounds good; then again, so does this; now this *really* does it.

Yet, with all the pleasure stimulating my reasoning powers, some persistent unease kept coming between me and the entire enterprise, which soon—from Aristotle to Rawls—began to seem rather more like a board game, with the dice of recombinant moral consideration being rolled repeatedly, and repeatedly landing on one square or another of a grid of neatly idealized possibilities, with none of the moves adequately reflecting the distinctly unaesthetic struggle over moral judgment that one has with life on the ground. Then I remembered that Sandel famously enjoins his students to argue with him, and so I, as much of an amateur at political philosophy as any undergraduate, accept the invitation to grapple with theory in the flesh as well as in the abstract.

Let's go back to the Golden Rule. As I grew older, I saw—with a shock from which I don't think I ever recovered—that this Rule, while excellent in theory, was not workable in practice. Transgression was alarmingly ever-present. People simply could not accord each other the "justice" of treating one another as they themselves wished to be treated. Let me revise that. Forget people. It was *I* who couldn't help transgressing. With all the good will in the world, I soon came to see that I myself was a swamp of fears, fantasies, and defenses that caused me to forfeit the integrity needed to act with Golden Rule justice toward those around me. My temper was ungovernable; an aggravated sense of insecurity caused me, in exchange after exchange, relationship after relationship, year after year, to do exactly what the Rule said it was impermissible to do: I scorned and humiliated, I challenged and confronted, dismissed and discounted; suffered when I acted badly, but could not bring myself under control. The source of the transgression lay deep in the wounded unconscious: it commanded me. I loved many people in the abstract—felt for them, sympathized with them, romanticized them—but I could not give them the only thing that mattered: what Kant called "respect," the one basic recognition required to bypass that fatal sense of degradation. In short, the chaos within prevented me from *acting* as though others were as real to me as I was to myself, although in theory they were. And here we come to the crux of the matter.

It is this—the chaos within—that is hardly ever addressed in *Justice*; although it is this, precisely, that is responsible for the all-important gap between practice and theory. Within that gap lies life as we actually experience it, with peacemaking reason eternally in thrall to the emotional conflict that steadily undermines our ability to accord each other the required respect of acting as though others are as real to us as we are to ourselves.

Now that I am thinking about all this, I am remembering that in the early 1970s, when the second wave of the woman's movement began to gather steam in America, the crucial word at the center of my feeling intelligence was neither "equality" nor "justice," it was always "real." "Real" meant that I wanted only to be born into the same existential unhappiness that afflicts all who take their social and political reality for granted. Suddenly, I was stunned— insulted!—by the realization that political history, from antiquity on, had withheld the recognition of that "reality" from whole classes of people, including women and—as though I'd become the doctor in Chekhov's "Ward Six," the man who comprehended the horrors of imprisonment only when he himself was imprisoned—could only *now* grasp what that insult signified. It was the existential need of our souls to *not* put ourselves in the place of another; to make hierarchies that would include and exclude; declare this group fully human and that one not; as though a sense of one's own reality *depended* on the lesser reality of another. And indeed. As Virginia Woolf asked, how could men dress up, speechify, go out and civilize the natives if they couldn't come home and see themselves writ twice as large as life in the eyes of their adoring wives?

It seems to me that of all the philosophers we encounter in *Justice*, John Rawls comes closest to understanding and taking into consideration the nature of our shared psychic disability; and seeks to counter it with precisely those measures that might close the gap between practice and theory. But even Rawls cannot speak adequately to the fact that political history, from classical times on, reflects our fear not of one another but of ourselves, projected onto one another.

Inevitably, a tide of emotional bewilderment overcomes us when we are made to realize that no matter how sophisticated the theory gets, the mystery remains of how to safeguard the necessary sense of self-worth—every human being's birthright—that we continually outrage, just by being ourselves. I am grateful to *Justice: What's the Right Thing to Do?* for having forced me to think again about that which I once thought I would never stop thinking.

13

Primo Levi

When Primo Levi committed suicide in 1987, many thought that he'd killed himself because his wartime imprisonment in Auschwitz had at last made it impossible for him to go on living; many others (this writer among them) believed that if it hadn't been for Auschwitz, Levi would have killed himself years earlier—that the war, in fact, had lengthened his life because the experience of the concentration camp gave him writing, and it was writing alone that controlled the life-threatening anxiety against which he had struggled from earliest youth. Bearing witness to the historic catastrophe of Nazi Germany allowed (nay, commanded) Levi's inner agitation to retreat far enough and long enough to let him exercise the talent for philosophical observation that had always been his but, until the war, had been without sufficient content to find form. It was Auschwitz that freed Levi to become the artist he so clearly was, and writing about it held his inborn despair in check for a good forty years; only then did it fail to win the day.

Primo Levi was born in the northern Italian city of Turin in 1919, into a family of secular, middle-class Jews who had been living in the Piedmont for generations. He grew up in one of the city's Jewish neighborhoods surrounded by aunts, uncles, grandparents, friends, and neighbors, most of whom remained solidly in place until World War II and, since most of them survived the war, even long after. Levi too. Except for a year in Milan, a year in Auschwitz, and another year spent getting back to Turin, he lived and died in the apartment in which he was born. When he married in 1947, it was to a girl from the neighborhood, and she readily agreed to move into the building and share the family flat with his sister and widowed mother. At the time of his death—he leaped from the third floor into the open stairwell of this very building—his grown son was living across the hall, his daughter a few blocks away, and his boyhood friends on the streets all about. As Levi himself said, Auschwitz was his only adventure.

He grew up physically small, intellectually gifted, emotionally nervous—possessed of (or by) a trembling insecurity that did not abate with the passage of time. People who knew Levi in his youth have testified to one biographer after another that his timidity was his torment. He wanted the world but did not dare leave home; he fantasized himself a visionary physicist but settled for industrial chemistry; fell rapturously and repeatedly in love but only from the waist up: sex terrified him. This last was surely the enduring bane of his existence.

In his twenties Levi was often infatuated, and the inability to approach a woman made him desperate. "I thought myself condemned," he wrote years later in the "Zinc" chapter of *The Periodic Table*, "to a perpetual masculine solitude, denied a woman's smile forever, which I nevertheless needed as much as air." And in the "Phosphorus" chapter, he wrote that looking into the future, he saw this morbid shyness as "a condemnation without appeal which would accompany me to my death, confining me to a life poisoned by envy and by abstract, sterile, and aimless desires." As late as 1975, he was writing as though this problematic condition had never been corrected.

Once, also in his twenties, Levi went mountain climbing with another chemist, a down-to-earth, unimaginative fellow whose joy in risk-taking during the climb was infectious; for Levi, scaling the mountain with this man was like eating of some exotic food of life. Of this incident, he wrote in middle age, "Now that many years have passed I regret that I ate so little of it, for nothing has had, even distantly, the taste of that meat, which is the taste of being strong and free, free also to make mistakes and be the master of one's destiny."

Throughout these trials and tribulations of the soul, Levi, when considering the major elements of his identity, inevitably thought of himself as an Italian, a chemist, a would-be writer, even a mountain climber and a failed lover. Like most Italian Jews, who felt as assimilated before the war as the German Jews, Jewishness *per se* was last on his list. Even in 1929, when Mussolini signed an agreement with the Catholic Church that established Catholicism as the state religion and relegated all other religions to the status of "tolerated cults," Jews like Levi shrugged. Nine years later, however, in 1938, the race laws were passed and all Italian Jews were shocked when they lost their civil rights, property, positions in public office, and right to higher education. As Levi had matriculated a year earlier at the University of Turin, he was allowed to continue his studies in chemistry, and eventually received a compromised degree in 1941. "I had in a drawer an illuminated parchment on which was written in elegant characters that one Primo Levi, of the Jewish race, had been conferred a degree in Chemistry *summa cum laude* . . . A dubious document, half glory and half derision, half absolution and half condemnation." Now he knew that in the eyes of his government, he was to be stigmatized as a Jew, and shortly after that branded nothing but a Jew. Little could he have imagined that this turn of events would lead him to his great and abiding subject: the experience of finding oneself transformed into a creature unworthy of being treated like a human among humans.

In the fall of 1942, Levi was living in Milan in the company of seven other boys and girls from Turin. Mussolini had fallen and the Germans now occupied Italy; but the war, at that point, was still at a distance from these youthful anti-Fascists, who went on living from day to day with ironic contempt for the regime but no real sense of urgency: "We went to the theatre and concerts and accepted with irresponsibility the nightly bombing by the English," Levi recalled, as the bombs weren't meant for *them*, they thought, but for the Germans. However, in November 1942 the Allies landed in North Africa, and in December began the Russian resistance in Stalingrad. "In the space of a few weeks each of us matured." Now, when "out of the shadows came men whom Fascism had not crushed . . . we recognized in them our teachers."

Soon enough, the virginal *summa cum laude* and his not much more experienced comrades went up into the mountains to join the partisans, although none of them knew the first thing about soldiering: "[Our mentors] had taught us that our mocking ironic intolerance was not enough . . . but they did not teach us how to make bombs or shoot a rifle." Within months, Levi's encampment was raided by the Fascist police, which turned its entire population over to the Germans. By February 1944, nearly every one of these twentysomethings was in Auschwitz.

The British critic John Gross, in reviewing Levi's *The Drowned and the Saved* in 1988, wrote: "The guards and the prisoners in the camps had at least one thing in common. Both groups knew that by the standards of the outside world, what they were taking part in was incredible. Even if someone lived to tell the tale, who was going to believe him?"

In later years, Levi said that he counted himself lucky to have been caught in 1944 because by then, although the daily selections for death were still in operation, the Germans were more concentrated on slave labor than on liquidation. What they never reduced their interest in, however, was the application of what Levi called "useless violence": administering blows and curses for no reason; withholding food and drink for no reason; ordering prisoners to stand naked in the yard for no reason ("in the blue and icy . . . dawn . . . all our clothing in our hands"). At first, Levi writes, "It was so new and senseless that we felt no pain . . . only a profound amazement: how can one hit a man without anger?"

Why? is the question that the twenty-four-year-old Primo—a child of the Enlightenment, committed to the rule of reason—kept asking himself. "Why would the Germans add humiliation and torment" to every hour of one's existence "when the final goal of murder was already fixed?" He knew that "our language lacks words to express this offence, the demolition of a man," but the Primo Levi who had trembled before women now stood remarkably alert before the Nazis, and was becoming a man who would spend the rest of his life absorbed by an experience for which there would never be enough of the right words.

Once in the camp, Levi quickly realized that what he was witnessing was the phenomenon of men having to reduce other men to the subhuman so that they could go on killing without themselves becoming deranged; and analogously, what it meant, as a prisoner, to fight (or seek) derangement while waiting to be killed. Then he realized there was more to it than that—much more. The situation was that of the boy pulling the wings off the fly in order to see how it was put together; the Nazis were the boy, the Jews the fly, and Auschwitz the "laboratory" of dissection. Why one set of human beings had brought themselves to thus treat another set of human beings was something he could not explain, but how it was being done he found he could—in incidents both dramatic and homely—describe brilliantly.

In a single famous incident in his memoir *If This Is a Man* (published in English as *Survival in Auschwitz* in *1959*), Levi writes that he was brought before an SS officer who was to decide whether he could be put to work as a chemist in the Auschwitz rubber factory. The officer is sitting at his desk, writing, when Levi is admitted to his office:

> When he finished writing, he raised his eyes and looked at me.
>   From that day I have thought about Doktor Pannwitz many times and in many ways ... [W]hen I was once more a free man, I wanted to meet him again, not from a spirit of revenge, but merely from a personal curiosity about the human soul ...
>   Because that look was not one between two men; and if I had known how to explain the nature of that look, which came across the glass window of an aquarium between two beings who live in different worlds, I would also have explained the essence of the great insanity of the Third Germany.

After his meeting with Dr. Pannwitz, Levi is taken back to his barrack by Alex the Kapo.

Suddenly, Alex loses his balance and reaches out to a cable running along the road to steady himself. When he takes his hand away, it is blackened by grease. "Without hatred and without sneering," Levi writes, "Alex wipes his hand on my shoulder, both the palm and the back of the hand, to clean it; he would be amazed, poor brute, if someone told him that today, on the basis of this action, I judge him and Pannwitz and the innumerable others like him, big and small, in Auschwitz and everywhere."

The German plan to reduce the Jews to a state of animal cunning succeeded to a frightening degree. Levi shuddered both during and after the war at the often astonishing behavior of his fellow prisoners. Once, after what proved to be the final selection for the gas chamber, a man in his hut fell to his knees thanking God out loud that he had not been chosen, even though a man lying in the bunk above him had been. Of this incident, Levi wrote, "If I was God, I would spit at Kuhn's prayer."

Nonetheless, Levi could understand the Kuhns all around him: "In the Lager . . . the struggle to survive is without respite, because everyone is desperately and ferociously alone . . . If [one] vacillates, he will find none to extend a helping hand; on the contrary, he'll be knocked aside, because it is in no one's interest that there will be one more" of the weak, the inept, those doomed to selection, taking up space.

What Levi would never understand was the willing remove of the Germans from their own fellow humanity. The ability to look—for years on end—at a human being and see not a person but a thing became and remained for Levi the crime of crimes. Yet for this, he very nearly blamed not the Germans but life itself. After all, if thousands upon thousands of people were capable of not seeing themselves in others, could this capacity be anything other than innate? Life itself, he concluded, was to be pronounced guilty for having made possible such a monstrous divide within the

human organism. This pronouncement became the unyielding reindictment—enlarged upon many times in books,
essays, and stories—that made Primo Levi one of the greatest of the Holocaust writers. As Berel Lang, Levi's newest
biographer, puts it in *Primo Levi: The Matter of a Life*,
"That someone who was himself" struggling to remain
human was "capable at the same time of recognizing and
reflecting on" the existential meaning of his incarceration
"makes Levi's work distinctive both as philosophy and as
history and memoir."

Lang is an emeritus professor of philosophy at SUNY
Albany who has written widely on the Holocaust. His book
on Levi is an intellectual biography characterized by a
somewhat schematic set of speculations on some of the basic
elements of Levi's life, each one arranged around the central
experience of Auschwitz. Among the questions Lang
ponders: If it wasn't for Auschwitz would Levi have written
at all? If it wasn't for Auschwitz would he have become a
self-conscious Jew? If it wasn't for Auschwitz would he have
killed himself? The book begins with the question of Levi's
suicide, which Lang rightly says is almost always the first
thing people talk about when Levi's name comes up. Here
is a random example of how Lang proceeds:

> The cause of death was judged to be a fall from the
> landing of Levi's apartment on the third floor . . . There
> were no witnesses . . . The verdict of suicide was thus an
> inference . . .
>
> [C]laims attributing Levi's suicide to his months in
> Auschwitz surfaced quickly

As Elie Wiesel wrote, "Levi died at Auschwitz forty years later."

Lang continues:

> Those who dissented entirely from the verdict of suicide . . . claimed (and still continue to hold) that for Levi to commit suicide would diminish or contradict too much else in his life and work, what he had lived through and for . . . he *should not* have done it or, more strongly, he *could not* have done it . . .
>
> Neither personal relationship nor independent analysis can fully settle the issue, although each item of evidence may add to or subtract from a conclusion in different measures . . .
>
> Some of his readers have argued that to accept the verdict of Levi's suicide . . . would undo the intellectual and emotional strength credited to Levi as survivor and witness.

Around each of these assertions Lang gathers a prodigious amount of rumination that includes his thoughts on suicide in general, Levi's in particular, and those of the imagined reader. Each of the chapters that follows treats Levi's relation to another of the aspects previously named—writing, thinking, Jewishness—in the same manner.

Lang's book does not represent an introduction to the life of Primo Levi. If the reader is expecting to find Levi, the flesh-and-blood man, on the page, he is not here. What *is* here is a philosophically minded investigation into the contextual nature of Levi's life, mainly as a prisoner of

Auschwitz. It asks: under what conditions does suicide represent a "free death"? How does the mind of a trained scientist come to a prisoner's aid? How does the visceral experience of the camp differ from the intellectual act of thinking about it?

Levi was undeniably himself in Auschwitz, but he was also like those hysterics who become commanding figures in the face of true crisis, when some previously untested essence within them is brought to life. In the concentration camp, a force greater than the fears that had routinely plagued him asserted itself. It was the force of the seriously stunned humanist who, trapped in an "end of civilization" scenario, looks into the void where the human condition in all its beauty, horror, and waywardness is expiring, and knows that should he live, he will be ordained to spend the rest of his days describing the unimaginable and the indescribable.

Ironically enough, it was precisely because Levi remained as human in the camp as he had been outside it that the person he had been before the war was there, waiting to claim him, no sooner was he once more a "free" man. Slowly, the old fears, anxieties, and depressions seeped helplessly back into his core being. That he kept them from closing in long enough to become one of the great tellers of those tales that warrant rewriting the Bible is nothing less than remarkable.

14

Hannah Arendt

Born a Jew destined to endure the catastrophe of Nazi Germany, Hannah Arendt experienced firsthand the despair inflicted on an entire civilization when the country of her birth consumed a continent in its determination to rule the known world. She saw, up close, something of the human condition writ large that organized her intellectual talent for the rest of her life. The experience made Arendt a political thinker.

She'd thought of herself as a Jewish German, not a German Jew. When the Nazis came to power, and friends, colleagues, neighbors scrambled to forget they'd ever known her, the transformation of her identity stunned her and the question of how it had come about became an obsession. True, political gangsters had hijacked Germany; but very quickly, it seemed, other European nations had adopted an equally open policy of official anti-Semitism, as though they'd only been waiting for the opportune moment. Why? And why now? The conviction among the Jews themselves that they were, as ever, only the regulation victims of the newest barbarians did not satisfy. For Arendt, this was an inadequate explanation for the immensity of what was happening.

The Jews, she knew, had for centuries accepted routine European anti-Semitism as a given, one that naturally precluded all worldly concerns except that of survival. Now, Jew-hatred had evolved into a political policy that forbade even the right to survive. She was persuaded that these elements were fused; the one, she came to believe, had not in fact been possible without the other. From there to the conviction that political freedom comes only with political responsibility—it's either earned or forfeited—was one easy step.

The Jewish Writings is a collection of Arendt's articles and essays written between 1932 and 1966. They come as a revelation. I had never understood, exactly, the mental road that Arendt had traveled to get to the pronouncements for which she has been both celebrated (the reality of men trumps the concept of Man), and damned (evil was ordinary; the Jews were to be held accountable). To read the book straight through is to see clearly the origin and steady development of the single critical insight that informed much of Arendt's subsequent work: namely, that the world is what we ourselves make it. The need to breathe free is a given; the right to do so is not. Among human beings, the will to power is an embodied force that continually challenges the right of those not like ourselves to occupy space. Under no conditions is the one not-like-oneself free to ignore the challenge. What's more, the challenge must be resisted in the terms in which it is flung down. As Arendt put it, "When one is attacked as a Jew one must respond not as a German or a Frenchman or a world citizen, but *as a Jew.*"

The Jewish preoccupation with simple survival had led to a peculiar kind of worldlessness (Arendt's word). Jews as Jews had long accepted the absence of all political action in their lives, adapting themselves skillfully to whatever circumstance was available to them, with the single shared intent of living as though gentiles did not exist. As that came down to the pursuit either of religiosity or of moneymaking, the mass of Jews lived in *shtetl* obscurity practicing a self-mesmerized worship of God's Law, while a few grew wealthy enough to bankroll the kings and ministers in whose regimes they had neither influence nor interest. This lack of worldly involvement led religious and secular Jews alike to become naively devoted to the conviction that Jews were outside of history (what Arendt means by "worldlessness"), and therefore—though they might be harassed, restricted, even murdered—would essentially be ignored. When the Nazis rose to power in Germany, charging a Jewish world conspiracy as the source of the Weimar Republic's miseries, they were thunderstruck, but greeted the accusation as no more than another chapter in the familiar history of anti-Semitic scapegoating.

What the Jews had failed to understand, Arendt now thought, was that there is no such thing as absenting oneself from history. If one is not an active participant in the making of one's world, one is doomed to be sacrificed to the world in which one lives. At all times, agency is required. To not exercise agency is, inevitably, to be enslaved by those who do exercise it. The former condition, in fact, stimulates the latter.

It was the acceptance of the unacceptable that Arendt now considered a crucial contribution of the Jews to their own undoing. That they had gone on living for centuries motivated only by the desire to protect their backs and shield their faces had increased the enmity, among governments and individuals alike, of those who saw in such meekness everything they feared and hated in themselves, if not in human existence. The Jews had never realized that what had been required of them was militant struggle against their subordinated status; without such struggle they were destined to remain social pariahs, integrated into Europe's economic life but actively despised within its culture. Here was a dramatic illustration of the inborn human impulse to bully, squash, destroy that which is cowed into subordination. In our own time, we have seen the liberationist movements of persecuted blacks, humiliated gays, discarded women take the historical lesson: when politically despised, you either fight on your feet or die on your knees.

Many of the pieces in *The Jewish Writings* of Hannah Arendt were originally published in *Aufbau,* a New York–based German-language newspaper for which Arendt wrote between 1941 and 1950, and they give us a Hannah Arendt many of us did not know existed: urgent, eloquent, advocating. One of the most recurrent elements in the book, for example, is her passionate insistence, throughout the Second World War, that the Jews of the world should mount their own army and fight Hitler with guns in their hands and righteousness in their hearts. She meant this literally. There were, of course, Jews fighting in the armies of all the allied forces—American, British, Russian—but they were not the point. The Jews had to fight Hitler under their own flag. "We must enter this war as a European people," she said, "who have contributed as much to the glory and misery of Europe as any other of its peoples." If the allied forces defeated Hitler for the Jews, it would do the Jews as a people no good at all because "from the disgrace of being a Jew there is but one escape—to fight for the honor of the Jewish people as a whole." Interestingly enough, an underground Polish newspaper tipped its hat to the Warsaw Ghetto uprising with these words: "The passive death of Jews had created no new values; it had been meaningless; but [this] death with weapons in hand can bring new values into the life of the Jewish people." In mid-twentieth century, it transpired, one earned the right to live in much the same way as one had when crouching in a cave.

Perhaps the most important running theme in these pieces is that the Nazi assault on the Jewish people was a major setback for Western civilization as a whole: Hitler's war had reduced to spiritual rubble modernity's one-hundred-and-fifty-year effort to honor the rights of individual human beings more than those of the state. Arendt was to consult this insight, written on her skin, for the rest of her life. In

1942 she wrote that German destruction of the European world of nations had begun with the destruction of the German nation itself "which has perished in the infamy of Dachau and Buchenwald." The same, she said, went for France: "When Petain put his signature to the infamous paragraphs of the French-German armistice, which demanded that every refugee in France be handed over to the Nazis, [he] tore the tricolor to shreds and annihilated the French nation." What was left in each country, she said, was only a shattered people battling for mere animal survival, having lost most of what made life worth living. Reading these words of Arendt's today, feeling as I and a few million other Americans do about our own country, it is painful to reflect on how much people long to believe in national honor and decency, how great a *political* need that longing addresses.

Arendt turned Jewish persecution on its head and demanded Jewish resistance not for the sake of the Jews alone, but for that of the entire modern world. In support of this position, she invoked the words of the French Zionist, Bernard Lazare, who, living in the France of the Dreyfus period, had urged Jewish rebellion against pariahdom because it was "the duty of every human being to resist oppression," not for one's own good, but for the good of all mankind. She might also have invoked Gandhi who, at the height of his iconic struggle for Indian independence, wrote in his journal: "The very right to live accrues to us only when we do the duty of the citizenship of the world."

This idea of responsible world citizenship became key for Arendt. It led her to the passionate conviction that the sovereign state must come to an end, as nationalism in the twentieth century had, clearly, proved itself the enemy of humanity. The state, she thought, should give way to federated commonwealths, each composed of a system of local governments—townships, councils, soviets—within which majorities and minorities would no longer be accorded differential rights. Such a system would facilitate the grass-roots practice of direct democracy, whereby "freedom will consist of political action among equals." A utopian vision, no doubt, but one held by social revolutionists like the anarchists, who had repeatedly made use of the vision to think hard about what human beings need to feel human.

The idea of a Jewish state appalled her. She had considered Palestine a homeland for the Jews, but never advocated carving out Jewish sovereignty at the expense of the Arabs already living on the land. For Arendt, first-class citizenship for Jews, and second-class for Arabs, was a horrifying prospect. She could not believe that the Jews were going to do to others what had been done to them—that the pariah-turned-rebel of whom she had dreamed would emerge from hell not a statesmanlike sage but a nationalist and a terrorist—and she opposed the formation of Israel from day one. This opposition took her to a place in her mind she had never imagined herself occupying.

In 1950 Hannah Arendt, who had spent so many years writing out of Jewish despair, wrote: "The Jews are convinced that the world owes them a righting of the wrongs of two thousand years and, more specifically, a compensation for the catastrophe of European Jewry which, in their opinion, was not simply a crime of Nazi Germany but of the whole civilized world. The Arabs, on the other hand, reply that two wrongs do not make a right and that no code of morals can justify the persecution of one people in an attempt to relieve the persecution of the other." Throughout the war, speaking as a Jew among Jews, Arendt had consistently written "we Jews." From now on, when writing about the Middle East, she would refer to both parties as "they." She was still passionate about the Jews— "the wrong done by my own people grieves me more than wrong done by other peoples"—only now the passion, instead of glowing red hot, burned like dry ice. Many of the things Arendt said in the '50s and '60s she had, in fact, said before, but the way she now framed them seemed to leave the Jews themselves behind. And very shortly, many Jewish readers returned the compliment.

The publication of *Eichmann in Jerusalem* in 1963 brought down on her—from every quarter of the western earth, it seemed—the open charge of Jewish self-hatred. The chief complaint against the book was Arendt's unsentimental account of the wartime European Jewish Councils' misguided attempt to buy time by cooperating with the Nazis and helping to draw up lists of people destined for deportation to the camps. Ironically, in 1937 Arendt had written "It seems to me that our political and spiritual leaders have done almost irreparable damage, [clouding] our vision of the larger historical context in which we stand, and into which we are dragged deeper and deeper day by day." This, she had added, was tantamount to signing one's own death warrant: a thing one must never do. At the time, patriarchal Jewry received these admonitions as though coming from an overly critical daughter whose loyalty was nonetheless desired. In 1963 the remoteness in Arendt's voice made clear that she invoked the Jews to illustrate concerns that went far beyond the subject of Jewry—and it was her head that was wanted. Among those who objected forcefully to the book was the Israeli scholar Gershom Scholem, who wrote Arendt a much-publicized letter, complaining bitterly of the book's coldness, and accusing her of having "no love of the Jewish people."

It was true, she replied: she had no love of the Jewish people. She had, she said, never loved "any people or collective—either the German people, nor the French, nor the American, nor the working class or anything of that sort." She had loved her friends; the only kind of love she knew was for that of persons. As for being Jewish, she went on, the one thing that did matter to her—and mattered vitally—was that being a Jew had been a given in her life. Not only had she never wished to be anything else, but being Jewish had made her appreciate, as nothing else could have, the significance of being allowed to be what one is: "There is such a thing as a basic gratitude for everything that is as it is: for what has been *given* and not *made*."

This regard for the givens of individual human existence had made her think deeply about everything she had thought mattered during the previous thirty years. What she loved was the *experience* of the Jewish people: it had taught her how to consider the human condition at large.

How much more Jewish did she have to be?

15

Erich Fromm

No sooner had the fighting of World War II ended than the Cold War began and the United States seemed plunged once more into the anxiety that had prevailed while the guns were firing. A manipulated terror of godless Communism, coupled with an even greater one of nuclear war, made the 1950s a decade in which ordinary women and men feared to speak freely or act independently. Injected into this unhealthy atmosphere was a straitjacket demand for conformity to what was rapidly becoming corporate America. In a world that had just fought one of the bloodiest wars in history for the sake of the individual, millions were rushing into the kind of lockstep existence that by definition meant a forfeiture of inner life.

Books written by sociologists, novelists, and psychologists describing this cultural turn of events were suddenly thick on the ground: David Riesman's *The Lonely Crowd* (1950),

Harry Stack Sullivan's *Interpersonal Theory of Psychiatry* (1953), Sloan Wilson's *The Man in the Gray Flannel Suit* (1953), and in some ways the most penetrating of all, Richard Yates's *Revolutionary Road*, a novel published in 1961 but set in 1955. It was a time, Yates claimed, that embodied "a kind of blind, desperate clinging to safety and security at any price."

The book, however, that accounted most fully for the 1950's near-morbid desire for security at any price had been written a decade earlier by the émigré psychoanalyst Erich Fromm. *Escape from Freedom* (1941), rooted in a European intellectual thought that had been heavily influenced by the work of both Karl Marx and Sigmund Freud, brought social psychology to the United States where, in the years ahead, it flourished wildly. The book launched its author on one of the most celebrated careers that any public intellectual, anywhere, has ever achieved.

Erich Fromm was born in 1900 in Frankfurt, Germany, into a lower-middle-class Jewish family that was nominally Orthodox. While Fromm never became religious, very early he fell in love with Judaism's great book of wisdom, and for years wished only to become a student of the Talmud. At the same time, on the verge of teenaged life, he came under the influence of an employee of his father, who introduced him to the work of Karl Marx. Then came the First World War which, in later years, Fromm labeled "the most crucial experience of my life." His newest biographer, historian Lawrence J. Friedman, tells us in *The Lives of Erich Fromm: Love's Prophet* that when the war was over the eighteen-year-old Fromm remained "obsessed by . . . the wish to understand the irrationality of human mass behavior." By Fromm's own accounting, these three strands of influence—Talmudic ethics, Marxist socialism, and the psychological power of unreason—shaped his intellectual life.

In 1919 he entered the University of Heidelberg where he studied under Max Weber's brother, Alfred, also a sociologist. Alfred Weber was convinced that while Freud's discovery of the strength of instinct drives rooted in sexuality was undeniable, more important was the social reality in which the individual life was planted. Weber persuaded the young Fromm that social forces working on the psyche were the key to what most troubled the human condition.

Nonetheless, Fromm also saw that to understand the workings of the psyche was vital. At the age of twenty-two he became a patient of Frieda Reichmann—a psychoanalyst ten years his senior who later became his first wife—and soon began to study analytic theory himself. He proved so precocious a student that by 1923 he was a practicing psychoanalyst in Berlin. In 1929 he became a lecturer and founding member at the Institute for Psychoanalysis at the University of Frankfurt. In Frankfurt, he quickly discovered that it was only Freud threaded through Marx that ignited his intellectual imagination; and he soon deserted one Frankfurt Institute for another: the Institute for Social Research that eventually gained international fame as the Frankfurt School of Critical Theory.

The Frankfurt School had been founded in 1922 by a wealthy Marxist who wished to see a body of research concentrated on the organized working class. By the end of the decade, however, a neo-Marxist development within the intellectual left was guiding the work of the Institute toward an exploration of the cultural rather than economic consequences of capitalism. It was this movement—led by scholars and critics like Max Horkheimer, Theodor Adorno, Walter Benjamin, Herbert Marcuse, and Leo Löwenthal— that established the Institute's originality. When, around 1929, a group of psychoanalysts that included Fromm and Wilhelm Reich was recruited (mainly by Horkheimer), the Institute was given the grounding in neo-Freudian thought that—together with cultural Marxism—became its signature trait.

During those early years at the Frankfurt School, Fromm wrote a multitude of essays that joined the basic principles of psychoanalysis to those of historical materialism, analyzing instinctual drives and needs in relation to the overriding sense of alienation brought on by modern capitalism. These essays were the genesis of *Escape from Freedom*, the work that identified *the* existential drama of the human condition: the will at one and the same time to break loose from the constraints of social authority and to submit to them. It was the rise of Nazism—the incredible ease with which Hitler made his way to power first in Germany and then in Austria—that amazed Fromm and made clear to him that humanity at large was almost always drawn to the infantile comfort of having an external authority make all the decisions.

Overnight, it seemed, millions of people, indifferent to the loss of democracy, were happy to capitulate to the rule of the strongman, relieved to feel order restored when they were being told what they could and could not do, no matter the human cost. This was a crisis that, in Fromm's view, threatened "the greatest achievement of modern culture—individuality and uniqueness of personality."

Why was this happening? What was it in the human psyche that welcomed what Fromm could only think of as a return to tribalism? The more he thought about it, the more clearly he saw that in all human beings a tug of war persisted between the desire to have freedom and the desire to shun its responsibilities. Friedman calls the latter "conformist escapism."

It was Fromm who saved the Institute from the Nazis. During a 1933 trip to the United States he persuaded Columbia University to give the Institute refuge, and a year later a large contingent of its membership—including Horkheimer, Adorno, and Marcuse—arrived in New York City, just one step ahead of certain arrest: not only were most of the Institute members Jewish, their ideas were anathema to National Socialism. It was then that Erich Fromm's life took its significant turn. While most of the Institute members continued to write in German for a select readership, Fromm instantly fell in love with America, the English language, and his own growing desire to become a social critic capable of reaching a wide reading public.

Over the next forty years he would write some twenty-five books, give thousands of lectures, join the Culture and Personality movement started by the anthropologists Margaret Mead and Ruth Benedict, become—along with the neo-Freudians Sullivan and Clara Thompson—a founding member of the William Alanson White Institute of

Psychiatry in New York, and establish a psychoanalytic section at an important university in Mexico, all the while maintaining his own clinical practice in New York and publishing, year after year, the steady stream of books and papers about authority and the individual self that made him immensely rich and famous. When he died in 1980, a few days short of his eightieth birthday, Fromm was one of the most influential public figures in the Western world.

Fromm's thesis in *Escape from Freedom* was a simple one and, like Freud before him, he did not hesitate to use the conventions of mythic storytelling to make it vivid for the educated layperson. In Freud's case the story derived from the classics; in Fromm's, from Genesis (don't forget those Talmudic studies). Human beings, he argued, were at one with nature until they ate of the Tree of Knowledge, whereupon they evolved into animals endowed with the ability to consciously reason and to feel. From then on they were creatures apart, no longer at one with a universe they had long inhabited on an equal basis with other dumb animals. For the human race, the gifts of thought and emotion created both the glory of independence and the punishment of isolation; on the one hand the dichotomy made the race proud, on the other, lonely. The loneliness proved our undoing. It so perverted our instincts that we became strangers to ourselves—the true meaning of alienation—and thus unable to feel kinship with others.

And it is just here that Fromm and Freud part company in a way that accounts for the vital difference between social psychology and hard-worked analysis. For Freud, the all-important loneliness of mankind was inborn; for Fromm it was culturally created. Freud said the conflict of instinctual drives means that human beings are born into a sense of loss and abandonment that can be ameliorated only through psychoanalysis. Fromm said it was enough to understand that the race is born with a sense of connectedness that is destroyed by the social climate.

Ironically, though, for each of these thinkers, it was the exercise of the very powers that had brought about our downfall that alone could release human beings from the imprisonment of such separateness. If men and women learned to occupy their own conscious selves, fully and freely, they would find that they were no longer alone: they would have themselves for company. Once one had company one could feel benign toward others.

This, Fromm said, was the only solution to the problem of the alienated individual in relation to the modern world. The only thing that could save humanity from its own soul-destroying loneliness was the individual's ability to inhabit what came to be known as one's "authentic" self. If you achieved authenticity, you would be rewarded with the inner peace necessary to become a free agent who is happy to do unto others as you would have others do unto you.

The fly in the ointment, as Fromm the Marxist saw it, was that we were living in a world where "economic, social and political conditions . . . do not offer a basis for the realization of individuality." That meant that the struggle to achieve authenticity was continually being so undercut that it became "an unbearable burden." If a burden is unbearable one will do almost anything to be relieved of it, even if relief demands submission to a set of social conventions that suffocates the spirit. This, however, is a Faustian bargain, one that creates anxiety. Now, something was needed to dull the anxiety. Capitalism, as Fromm and many other Frankfurt intellectuals said, had just the thing: consumerism. The pursuit of worldly goods—escapist conformism—would etherize the unrealized hunger for a genuine self.

Fromm dedicated his professional life—in increasingly popular form—to this thesis. On many fronts, that popularity did him in. To begin with, the Frankfurt intellectuals heaped scorn on him for being in love with concrete reduction when they were in love with abstract elaboration. Then he was faulted by psychoanalysts for distorting or dismissing many of the basics of Freudian analysis and then by social critics for recklessly urging on his readers the pursuit of naked self-interest. But his insights struck home with millions of people who, suffering from our famous American "emptiness" (especially in the 1950s) were happy to take the existential journey to emotional fulfillment that his ever more prophetic-sounding books steadily promised.

In *The Art of Loving* Fromm argued that the phrase "falling in love" was a dangerous misnomer. We did not fall into anything; what we did, once attraction had allowed a relationship to form, was recognize ourselves in the other and then—through affection, respect, and responsibility—work hard to teach ourselves how to honor that recognition. "Once one had discovered how to listen to, appreciate, and indeed love oneself," Friedman paraphrases *The Art of Loving*, "it would be possible to love somebody else . . . to fathom the loved one's inner core as one listened to one's own core." In short, the dynamic would induce an emotional generosity that allowed each of us to be ourselves in honor of the other. Once one had achieved this admittedly ideal state, Fromm declared, as he did in every single book he wrote, one could extend that love to all mankind.

Today, Fromm's thesis is so integrated into the therapeutic culture that it reads like a page out of a self-help book. That's how foolishly programmatic it can sound to the contemporary ear. But in the 1960s his masterwork, *Escape from Freedom*, helped politicize a generation of analysands and activists. With the aid of Fromm's book, these people gained a new grasp of the relation between historic injustice, psychological anxiety, and bourgeois reluctance to challenge the authority of outworn conventions even when an army of dissidents was gathering in the name of sacrificed individuality. Above all, Fromm's insights shed light on the age-old fear of equality for women, blacks, and gays, and helped those on the barricades resist the castigation of frightened conservatives who labeled the liberationist cause "the selfishness of the Me Generation."

Erich Fromm: Love's Prophet is not, strictly speaking, a biography. It is rather a very long summary of the twists and turns of Fromm's life as a public intellectual. But the man who had dinner with presidents, gave lectures for thousands, sold books in the millions—we know him no better at the end of three hundred–odd pages than we did at the beginning. We are told that in the opinion of the psychoanalyst Karen Horney, with whom he had an affair, Fromm exhibited a "self-righteous messianic or prophetic quality that limited" his capacity for "emotional sharing." We are told that he was an addicted womanizer, and, although *The Art of Loving* came out of a happy second marriage, the affairs never stopped. We are told that in his psychoanalytic practice he was more guru than analyst, demanding of his patients that they "awaken" to what he insisted were their "choices," the ones that would enable them "to become more spontaneous, joyful, exuberant, and productive." All these things we are told, but there is no more compulsion to believe than to disbelieve them, as there would be if the man at the center had come alive on the page.

However, Friedman's book is a thoroughly absorbing history of the cultural and political context within which Fromm's life was lived. We feel the intellectual turbulence of Europe in the 1920s; the exciting crisis of Nazism in the 1930s (nothing more exciting than evil developing right before your eyes), and then the cynical innocence of America in the 1950s. We also feel the meaning of a particular man and a particular world well met, with each imprinting memorably on the other.

It is now more than seventy years since *Escape from Freedom* was published, and we are living in a world where women and men feel neither safe, secure, nor, I daresay, authentic. We are, however, all of us, a thousand times more conscious than we were in 1941 of the fact that when we invoke those words—safe, secure, authentic—we are talking about a state of being that can never be handed us; it must be earned, from the inside out. For that sea change in the shared sensibility of the culture we have many influences to thank—among them, surely, the works of Erich Fromm.

16

The Americanization of Narcissism

I can remember as though it were yesterday, my jaw dropping when, in 1978, Christopher Lasch's *Culture of Narcissism* was published, and I discovered in its pages that as a radical feminist of long standing I qualified as a major narcissist of what the journalist Tom Wolfe had dubbed the "Me Decade." We, whose rallying cry was "Not for ourselves alone"? We, who hoped to see all future relations between men and women take place on a level playing field? We, who thought power over ourselves would mean we'd never want power over others? We were narcissists?

The Americanization of Narcissism, by the historian Elizabeth Lunbeck, is a deeply researched account of the long and complicated life the concept of narcissism has had among psychoanalysts, as well as its short, oversimplified one at the hands of the social critics who in the 1970s chose to make polemical use of it. As such, this book is by way of being a corrective. Its author seeks to rescue narcissism from the distortions she feels it has been subjected to by the critics who, instead of addressing the noisy discontent of their time with sympathetic interest, sought only to castigate it, and in the process did irreparable harm to any working definition of narcissism that was ever in analytic use.

"From the beginning," Lunbeck writes, "analysts used narcissism to account for the best and worst in us, to explain our capacities for creativity and idealism as well as for rage and cruelty, our strivings for perfection and our delight in destructiveness." In its fullest sense, narcissism is a complicated theory of human development that, to begin with, includes a description of the healthy selfishness that an infant or a youth demonstrates in seeking to stand on its own two feet. When one matures, this infantile selfishness drops away as one becomes an independent person with a proper respect for one's own needs as well as the needs of others. When the process goes off the rails, and there is a failure to mature, elements of primitive self-involvement linger on throughout one's adult years. Then, if a person is dominated by infantile self-absorption, we say they have narcissistic personality disorder.

In America, in the 1970s, two eminent analysts became famous for arguing the polarizing characteristics of narcissism—on the one hand it was normal, on the other pathological—and the analyst who argued for the pathological won the day. Heinz Kohut concentrated on the normalizing aspect of narcissism, describing it not as "navel-gazing" but rather as a means of attaining a healthy sense of self-esteem. As Lunbeck tells it, he "outlined a normal narcissism that was the wellspring of human ambition and creativity, value and ideals, empathy and fellow feeling . . . positively tinged, replete with possibility, and necessary to sustain life." Otto Kernberg, by contrast, described narcissism as a malignancy, a disorder of the kind that froze human empathy in its tracks. "Kernberg's clinical writing chronicles the deformation of human relatedness," Lunbeck explains, "presenting readers with an astonishing range of ways we as humans have devised to mistreat, exploit, and destroy one another—and ourselves."

It was the pathology of narcissism that drew the attention of analysts who—finding themselves stumped by patients whose ailments reflected the social confusion of the moment, and not knowing quite how to deal with it—were quick to characterize those who complained endlessly of an "inner emptiness" as victims of the disorder. And the times being what they were, social critics followed suit, immediately embracing Kernberg's point of view and marginalizing Kohut's. It was the critics who fed a confused nation, hungry for some oversimplification of the forces pulling its world apart, a definition that distorted the complexities of narcissism itself while sweeping legitimate discontent under the rug.

"Only by understanding the controversies around narcissism's organizing concepts," Lunbeck writes, "and only by appreciating how resonant with their own concerns social critics found these controversies, can we account for how eagerly narcissism was embraced and how readily it found a home in a nation that Freud thought so inhospitable to his science of psychoanalysis." The analysts themselves rejected the idea that society could produce either normal or pathological narcissism, considering the claim a desperate attempt to explain what Lasch called the "underlying character structure" of the age. But the critics would not be denied.

For Lunbeck, Lasch was the worst of these critics. His was the grossest misapplication of the concept of narcissism. It was through Lasch, Lunbeck writes, that in the 1970s "narcissism was cast as a pathology associated with worldly affluence and abundance, and remained so for thirty years, obscuring its roots" in a neurosis that could be traced only to an individual's unique sense of infantile deprivation. In the hands of Lasch and other critics, this neurosis, invariably to be located in the family of origin, became a product of social influences experienced as an adult.

Lunbeck's primary interest here is the intellectual history of narcissism and, as such, her book is mainly devoted to a taxonomy of its various definitional twists and turns among psychoanalysts through the decades since Freud first addressed the subject in 1914. But for this reader it is her rehearsal of the use and misuse of the term in the 1970s that is the richest part of her book. Not only is it immensely evocative of the times themselves, but it also traces beautifully the way a valuable concept that includes a necessary stage of human development became permanently identified as a personality disorder that swallowed whole the larger, far more generous idea of the self that had been developing in the West for fifty years and more, into which narcissism should only have been enfolded.

At the turn of the twentieth century, an indescribable restlessness born from decades of revolutionary uprising in

Europe began turning the Western world sharply away from the long-held conviction that human beings are creatures of reason and moral self-control with obligations rather than rights. In place of this outworn faith, the West moved toward a contemplation of people as creatures of feeling and instinct whom history had systematically ignored or denied. An enormous change—soon to be known as modernism—in how ordinary people were coming to view the development of their own lives was in progress. Chief among the influences driving this change was the work of Sigmund Freud, whose open lectures, then being given in Vienna, were electrifying all of Europe.

As every kind of authority—church, family, custom—was being called into question, the most basic articles of social faith began to loosen their hold. This development allowed for the entertainment of thoughts and emotions hitherto unthinkable. Suddenly, it was as though a pressing need for inner fulfillment seized hold of a culture previously given to restraint and repression, and an epic struggle was begun between the old-fashioned need for law and order and the newer-fashioned one for rights rights rights: workers wanted the right to unionize, women wanted the right to vote, everyone wanted the right to unmarried sex.

A sea change in human self-definition was taking place but its significance was beyond those who longed only for things to stay as they were. Instead of trying to understand what was happening and why, they chose to see the social chaos as criminal and to look for the villain on whom to lay the blame. Ah, they had one. It was the incredible, unheard of, never-before-seen selfishness—that is, the self-love—of this generation of reckless, childish people playing at revolution, refusing to grow up and assume its ordained responsibilities. There was your culprit!

Half a century later, the task of modernism hardly having been completed, this scene was to replay itself, but this time with a culprit more exotically named by those who once again wished for things to stay as they were. America in the 1960s was also a culture split down the middle and approaching an instability that promised implosion. Here you had a middle class that was the freest, richest, most educated in the world complaining bitterly of an inner emptiness that seemed engulfing. At the same time there was a stalled war in Vietnam where Americans were dying gratuitously, and a stalled civil rights movement at home where Americans were dying shamelessly. From this crisis there emerged the twin developments of the consciousness movement and the counterculture. Out of the consciousness movement came an army of therapists and writers of how-to and what-it-all-means books that is with us to this day. And out of the counterculture came the liberationist movements whose slogans echoed those of that earlier phase of modernism, only this time the rights that were wanted cut deeper than ever before.

Emboldened by fifty years of Freud and Marx, the counterculture laid claim to the time-honored American ideal of self-realization. Unexpectedly, it was women and homosexuals, more than any other class with its voice raised, who, politically speaking, came to embody the ideal. Under the influence of this powerful national discontent, women and gays had become aware of the second-class citizenship that characterized their lives and were now finding the courage to speak out, to insist that their irreducible humanity be recognized before the law and in social custom. Essentially, they were insisting that the republic honor its broken promise of full egalitarianism, and overnight, it seemed, they were out in the street in numbers that radicals found exhilarating, conservatives frightening. This time around, the keepers of a disintegrating culture had a more glamorous name for the cause of the disruption than mere selfishness: *narcissism!*

The negative application of the concept of narcissism was monolithic, though the life around us so full of contradiction. It was hard to know why so many critics allowed themselves to record only the abuses (and indeed there were many) of both the consciousness and the liberationist movements while ignoring the vital seeds of social change that were being planted amid all the hullabaloo.

It was Lasch who, more influentially than any of the others, beat the drum for America having become a society of middle-class consumers on the one hand and radical protesters on the other. Between them, they were like the malignant, fantasy-ridden children everyone knew narcissists to be, destroying the only thing that mattered: social stability.

And what was the essential form that social stability took for Lasch? The family. The family, he claimed, that "haven in a heartless world" for men such as himself, was more important than any argument for individuation that anyone could be making. Individuation, for Lasch, was narcissism. "To live for the moment is the prevailing passion," Lasch wrote, "to live for yourself, not your predecessors or posterity." Thus the women's movement in particular was doing untold damage to the family as we knew it. There was no doubt, he conceded, that the subjugation of women under the patriarchy that had made us all what were today was truly terrible. But, he concluded, yesterday's fiction of female helplessness and male protectiveness was useful. At the very least it insured a modicum of civilized behavior. Awful as it all was yesterday, Lasch seemed to be saying, it was better than it is today; the unspoken half of that sentence being, when papa got respect, and mama knew her place, and the kids didn't talk back.

Why, one wondered, did the critics not make a case for the liberationists as an exemplary instance of the "good" narcissism at work? Why did the critics not see that what, at that moment, looked like the selfishness of these thousands of women and gays out in the street was the selfishness, necessary to a politically adult independence, of one emerging from a long cultural childhood? By the same token, why, one also wondered, did they look to the worst of the consciousness movement (to all that was indeed foolish and half-baked in it) instead of to the best of it; to the fact that it contained large and powerful insights that were striking chords in countless young people struggling to lead serious lives; insights from which, historically speaking, there would be no turning back.

The subtitle of Lasch's book is "An Age of Diminishing Expectations." That, unfortunately, was the way the world looked to a white, middle-class man without the gift of empathy who found all the social tumult depressing rather than stimulating, and who, feeling the ground beneath his own feet beginning to give way, came perilously close to idealizing a solidity of the past that never was.

For better or worse, for political riches or social poverty, freedom in the past century was profoundly linked to the idea of self-discovery. For many of us, in the 1960s, civilization seemed to be reforming itself in miniature within each of us, not for the purpose of attaining self-absorbed privilege but, on the contrary, so that free adult beings might reach out to one another in strength rather than weakness. It seemed to me then and it seems to me now that this sense of new life within us—strong, vibrant, unruly—was like a weed pushing up through concrete. The point was to keep your eye on the weed. The critics had their eyes on the breaking concrete.

17

The Second Sex at Fifty

This year *The Second Sex* turns fifty. Now deep into my own middle age, I reread the book in the wake of thirty years of thought and feeling much influenced by its steady presence among us and I find, turning its pages, that the question on my mind is not, "How does it read?" but rather, "How did it get written?"

In the 1989 Vintage edition of *The Second Sex* de Beauvoir's biographer, Deirdre Bair, tells us that in the fall of 1946, when

Sartre was under sustained verbal attack in Paris . . . [de Beauvoir] believed she could defend [his] positions . . . by writing an essay in which she defined herself personally as a woman and philosophically as an existentialist. Her intention was to relate them both to Sartre's system, which she had accepted unquestioningly as her own

... In order to defend what she believed were Sartre's universal principles, she had to begin with the specific and the individual, which in this case was her role within his system ... One idea began "to emerge with some insistence" from her thinking. It brought her to "the very profound and astonishing realization" that she was different from Sartre "because he was a man and I was only a woman."

In a 1982 conversation, Bair goes on, "she explained what she meant by 'only'":

I had not yet settled on the idea of woman as the other—that was to come later. I had not yet decided that the lot of woman was inferior to the allotment of men in this life. But somehow, I was beginning to formulate the thesis that women had not been given equality in our society, and I must tell you that this was an extremely troubling discovery for me. This is really how I began to be serious about writing about women—when I finally realized the disparity in our lives as compared to men. But [in 1947], none of this was clear to me.

In 1947 none of this was clear to her. She was thirty-nine years old. She had been out in the world as Sartre's intellectual companion for twenty years. She knew everyone, went everywhere; experienced herself as a person who spoke, thought, and moved freely. But now, setting out to write a simple analysis of her own life that would demonstrate the truth of Sartre's philosophy, she found herself coming up against a stumbling block around which there seemed at first no easy way out—and then no way out at all. When it came right down to it, she realized, she was first and foremost a woman; that reality undercut almost everything she intended to demonstrate. It struck her forcibly that the condition carried more weight than she had previously been willing or able to understand. Throughout the history of the human race, she now saw, people who were women had systematically had less power, less standing, less definition. They were, in fact, what Existentialism called "Other." The condition of birth into which she herself had been born was the single most powerful determinant in the shaping of a life consigned to organized subordination. To not see this, the "otherness" of your life, if you were a woman, was to live in a permanent state of fantasy.

De Beauvoir came up against being a woman in much the same way as James Baldwin—in the same year, in the same city—came up against being black. Although Baldwin had scorned the intellectual torments of postwar Europe—after all, they'd brought it on themselves, hadn't they?—it was impossible to be living in Paris in 1948 and not absorb the endless discussion of existentialist categories. Baldwin, too, began to see that he was "Other"; and then he saw that the idea of the "Other" was something he could make use of; turn it this way and that to concentrate all the better, all the more exactly, on what it meant to be black. Conversely, de Beauvoir had begun by wanting to use herself only to make the case for Existentialism but had ended with a radically changed perspective that also concentrated itself on her own "otherness." In the case of Baldwin, this application of the "Other" led to some of the most extraordinary essays in American literature. In the case of de Beauvoir, it led to a monumental work of rediscovery that would, twenty years later, help usher in the second wave of Western feminism.

The story of how *The Second Sex* came to be written is in itself a prototypic tale of how modern feminism has proceeded to make use—every fifty years or so over the past two hundred years—of the conversion experience of one "brilliant exception" after another—starting with Mary Wollstonecraft in England, leading on to Elizabeth Cady Stanton in America, and then on to de Beauvoir herself in France. Each of these women began her thinking life as an ardent partisan of a powerful social movement connected with a great war (the Enlightenment, the antislavery movement, Existentialism), and each of them, living a heightened life inside the visionary politics that had sparked her intellectual being, came, in turn, to see that she was "only a woman." The contribution each then made to feminist understanding turned, appropriately enough, on an application of the central insight of the movement to which she was devoted. Wollstonecraft urged passionately that women become rational beings; Stanton that every woman exercise governance over her own inviolate self; de Beauvoir that women cease to be "Other."

Once de Beauvoir "got it" she became brilliantly, comprehensively obsessed: the more she read the more she thought; the more she thought the more she read. Her research was formidable, her concentration unparalleled. The picture widened and deepened, reaching back into biblical times, forward toward the end of her own century. How "woman became woman" began to encompass large notions of Destiny, History, and Myth-making; as well as even larger analyses of women in our own time as a group of people prepared from birth to become the Desired and the Protected, but never the Independently Acting. There had not, she observed, been a time when the social history of the human race did not posit man as the central actor on the stage of life and woman as his sidekick.

Why? She asked herself again and again—but could come up with no adequate answer to the question. Nothing—not biology, not materialism, not psychoanalysis—could explain to her satisfaction why woman had become the permanent subordinate of man. At last she concluded that the answer lay in the "imperialistic" nature of human consciousness. It craved subordination; wherever and whenever it could, it created the "Other" in order to oppress it. As good an explanation for that which can never be "explained" as any—and one that led her into a wealth of observation that, to this day, we do not tire of responding to. Whether with gratitude or outrage.

In English *The Second Sex* runs to more than seven hundred pages, in French many more (the English edition is famously cut). The book is a magnificent piece of obsession on the grand scale: every resentment hounded to earth again and again. ("I have seldom read a book that seems to run in such concentric circles," Alfred Knopf said of it. "Everything [is] repeated three or four times but in different parts of the text.") At the same time, the book is written in a tone of voice remarkably self-distancing. The author of *The Second Sex* is at pains to put space between herself and her subject. She knows the condition whereof she speaks intimately but make no mistake, reader, she does not share it. Women—in this book written by a woman of great intellect and equally great outrage—are distinctly "they" not "we."

The rub, for de Beauvoir, was what she saw as the collaboration of women in their own fate. Blacks had submitted, but women had complied. It was the complicity she found unbearable. Throughout history they'd been relaxing like a cat into the subordinate condition; more than relaxing; endorsing the arrangement, sharing in the conspiracy, stupidly happy to remain slaves. She could not associate to it. The whole thing made her ill. As ill as it made Doris Lessing, whose *Golden Notebook*—the other major work on women written in the first half of the century—is a catalogue of grievance and self-hatred also delivered in a voice of angry scorn that separates the one writing from the ones being written about. (If it comes to that, Mary Wollstonecraft, writing in 1796, is also in a rage at those whose long-withheld rights she is setting out to vindicate.) Yet how could it have been otherwise? For women like Lessing and de Beauvoir, women's rights was the intellectual ghetto. It is amazing enough that they delivered themselves of these encyclopedic accounts of the condition of their own sex. For them to have placed the materials of a woman's life at the center of serious works of intellect and sensibility was in itself an astonishment.

But it is interesting and important to note that the only American visionary thinker equal in intellectual stature to the Europeans—Elizabeth Cady Stanton—wrote "we" not "they" from the first minute she put pen to paper—it is not until "they" transmutes into "we" that you've got a movement—and that is why feminism belongs to America. Much as they burned over their second-class status, it was impossible for the European intellectuals—from Wollstonecraft to de Beauvoir—to give up their overwhelming longing for acceptance in the world of men (such was the strength of European culture internalized). This longing—erotic in its power to compel—bound them heart and soul to a dividedness of will that was crippling. The American visionaries, on the other hand, hardened their hearts against the romantic pull of worldliness—and eroticized feminism (such was the power of the democratic promise outraged). Women's rights became their single-minded passion. This made them incomparably more undivided in their pursuit of equality—and incomparably more revolutionary. Thus, although feminism is rooted intellectually in Europe it is only here in America that it takes hold and becomes a movement.

In 1947 de Beauvoir began a now famous affair with Nelson Algren. The affair came as a revelation for her. With Algren, she said, heart, soul, and flesh were one. She was alive in her senses as never before. It was the kind of feeling for which most people gladly "give up everything." But Simone de Beauvoir was not most people.

Just months into the affair Algren asked her to marry him and move to Chicago. Reluctantly, she refused him and explained,

The reason I do not stay in Chicago is just this need I always felt in me to work and give my life a meaning by working. You have the same need, and that is one of the reasons for which we understand each other so well. You want to write books, good books . . . I want it too. I want to convey to people the way of thinking which is mine and which I believe true. I should give up travels and all kinds of entertainments. I should give up friends and the sweetness of Paris to be able to remain forever with you; but I could not live just for happiness and love, I could not give up writing and working in the only place where my writing and work may have a meaning.

One way or another she repeated these words a number of times over the years, and when she did, she seemed often to be saying, "Give up Paris? Give up French? Give up Sartre?" Her severest critics pounce on this construction, as though it is proof that the most famous feminist of the century was, finally, just another woman in thrall to the Great Man. I find this reading appalling. What is true is that it's hard to pull those sentences apart. For her, I think, they actually were of a piece. Taken together they did define the tenet of faith she called work.

They were not good people, neither she nor Sartre—ruthlessly self-absorbed, sexual predators, always needing to exert power over those within their orbit—but they were passionate about the life of the mind, and for each of them, writing was a religion. Whatever else Sartre did to her or for her, the association with him was irrevocably bound up with the idea of work. Indeed, his presence in her life was iconic, and she seemed often to be worshiping the man himself. But I don't believe she was. Crudely put, in a bid for independence on the part of a woman born in France in 1908, devotion to one man promised joy of the body, devotion to another man joy of the mind. That was the best she could do. She made her necessary—her distinctive—choice.

And it seems to me it stood her in infinitely better stead to hold work rather than love as a first value. It made her a better human being (the same cannot be said for Algren, a thin-skinned man, easily humiliated, capable in his neediness of cruel and reckless raging). In her letters to Algren, de Beauvoir never whines, pleads, threatens, or insults; no matter what is happening between them, the letters open with love and close with warmth. Out of them can be intuited the woman who applied herself to the task of researching and writing a report on the condition of her own sex with so much passionate steadiness that she transformed a polemic into one of the great books of the century.

TWO NEW YORK STORIES

18

On the Bus

For many years I taught one semester a year in graduate writing programs, nearly all of them far from home. Some while ago I was offered a position at a state university two hundred miles from New York and, calculating quickly that from this distance I could commute, I accepted the job. Sure enough, things worked out as I had hoped they would, and I was able to come home every weekend. What I did *not* expect (or bargain for), was that I would be traveling to the school and back on a Greyhound bus. The university, as it turned out, was in the exact middle of nowhere. Like most New Yorkers, I don't own a car, and getting to it by train or plane was so roundabout and expensive a process that a four-and-a-half-hour bus ride proved the only realistic means of transportation.

The bus I took left the Port Authority Terminal in Manhattan six times a day bound for Cleveland, Chicago, and either San Francisco or Salt Lake City. On Monday I'd board it at five in the afternoon and be dropped at nine thirty in the evening at a truck stop fifteen miles from the school, where I'd be picked up and driven into town. On Thursday nights, I'd be returned to the truck stop at eight thirty in the evening, and be back in Port Authority at one in the morning.

Often I was the only one to leave or board the bus at this truck stop. Leaving New York, the other passengers were all headed for Cleveland or Chicago, although a significant number were setting out for the West Coast, often looking as exhausted at the start as they undoubtedly would be at the finish. The bus was, in fact, a study in exhaustion: a thing I came to realize only slowly. Most of my traveling companions were working-class blacks, or Latinos or Asians who didn't speak a word of English, and many of them were badly, even incoherently put together. But it wasn't the ragged dress code, as I at first thought, that gave the bus its derelict look. It was the exhaustion. The deracinating exhaustion.

It began in New York in the bowels of Port Authority, where people started "lining up" at the lower-level gate more than an hour before the bus was due to leave. Almost no one was actually standing. People slumped against the wall, or sprawled across a duffel bag, or sat cross-legged on the floor. As the line grew, and began to snake ever farther out and away from the gate itself, the lassitude of the crowd grew apace. A kind of low-grade melancholy began to seep into the atmosphere as the Asians were almost entirely silent, the blacks looked asleep on their feet, the Latinos sad and murmurous. The line soon began to resemble a crowd of refugees: people with no rights, only obligations. By the time the driver pushed open the door and started taking tickets everyone looked beaten.

It was always a surprise to me when I found one of the front seats empty. Although those seats were a special concern of mine—on a long trip it is my invariable pleasure to dream out the front window—by the time I arrived at the gate there were always twenty-five people ahead of me in line. There go the front seats, I'd sigh inwardly, but when I climbed the steps of the bus, more often than not, I'd find one of the four empty. Almost everyone ahead of me had made for the back. By the time we were loaded and ready to go, three out of five passengers were burrowed down in their seats, eyes closed, shoulders slumped, heads disappearing below the level of the backrest facing them.

Sometimes, however, I would have to settle into a seat farther back in the bus and quite often when I did—again to my surprise—the tired-looking person sitting next to me would start talking at me: how long was it gonna take to get this show on the road; never can make these recliners work; the leg room here is pathetic. I did not welcome these harmless openers because I knew that, almost invariably, they meant I'd soon be taken hostage. As I am compulsively sociable, it is impossible for me to turn a deaf ear or a closed face to someone speaking to me. Even though I usually end up wishing the earth would open up and swallow the one inflicting tedium on me, on my face there remains an attentive expression and out of my mouth, every now and then, comes an unavoidable "Really!" or "I know what you mean."

I have spent a fair amount of my life trapped by those who are boring me into a rage because once they start talking I am forced to listen. It was always remarkable to me on those Monday–Thursday Greyhound trips that the people talking at me never seemed to notice that I hardly said a word.

One Thursday night in the late fall of my second year at this school, I climbed on the bus at the truck stop and found a seat beside a woman sitting three rows back from the front. She was thin, with long blond hair framing a narrow face, wearing a teenager's tank top, mini skirt, and high-heeled white boots. Her head was propped against the backrest, her eyes closed, her body limp. She seemed drained to the point of illness. But as I sank down beside her she opened her eyes, turned, and very soon asked if I lived around here. "No," I said. "I don't." "You from New York?" she asked. "Yes," I said. "Nothing like the city," she said. I smiled. "I'm from Cleveland," she said. I nodded. "Ever been in Cleveland?" I shook my head no. "Don't bother," she said. I smiled again. "I live in New York but my mother's sick, so I'm back and forth between Cleveland and New York these days."

Her name was Jewel. Twenty years ago, right after high school, (make that twenty-five, I thought) she'd come to New York to become a stage actress. Things hadn't exactly worked out as she had planned, but she was one of the most sought-after extras for nearly every movie made in the city. She also worked as a bartender in midtown. Before we got to Port Authority Jewel told me that her mother was dying of cancer, her father was a sweet man who had a hard time making a decision, and her brother, a doctor, was keeping their mother alive by some pretty extraordinary artificial means.

A week later, I climbed on the bus, and there was Jewel again, sitting the same three rows back, with the same empty seat beside her. She signed to me, and I felt obliged to sit down next to her. She looked as worn out as she had the week before but, smiling warmly, she asked how my week had been, waited patiently for me to say okay, then launched herself. "I don't know," she began, "something doesn't feel right to me, it just doesn't feel right." I took a deep breath and said, "What do you mean?" "My brother," she said. "It's like he's *obsessed*." She talked steadily for the next two hours.

They'd been raised on a farm just outside of Cleveland, her father had never made a living, her mother had been cold to her and devoted to her brother. The brother was married and a father himself, but he seemed never to have felt for anyone what he felt for their mother. Of course, Jewel was just guessing. Nobody ever *said* anything in that family. But her brother and her mother *did* speak together every morning, and clearly each preferred the other's company to that of anyone else. When she got sick he cheerfully went to work to save her. There was no question of not finding a way. But she had not responded to any of the many treatments that had been tried. Now she was a bag of bones, and kept saying she thought it was time for her to go. "No, Ma," Jewel's brother kept saying. "Not yet. I can't let you go yet."

Between late October and Christmas of that year I sat on the bus every Thursday night listening to Jewel rehearse the latest episode in the family romance of the doomed mother and the entranced son. "You should see the two of them in the hospital room," she'd say. "They've got eyes for no one but each other. My father and I just sit there. We don't even look at each other. It's embarrassing. I keep thinking we've got no business watching them." Chekhov once said that people who travel lose all reserve; he must have had Jewel in mind.

I, meanwhile, said almost nothing. Week after week, I sat beside Jewel, my body turned toward her, my elbow on the armrest between us, fingers ridging up into either my right or my left temple, eyes trained on her face: nearly silent.

On the last Thursday of the semester I settled into the seat beside Jewel, and we pulled out into a cold, clear night made magical by the colored lights outlining the vast eighteen-wheelers dancing up or down the highway on either side of the bus. I let myself be mesmerized. Jewel rattled on—he was pulling her back from the grave, the other doctors thought he'd gone over the edge, his wife was on the verge of divorce—hardly noticing that I wasn't really there.

At one in the morning the driver steered the bus into its Port Authority berth and turned on the inside lights. Everyone in front stood at once, picking up packages, putting on coats. I stepped into the aisle just behind Jewel. As we approached the door she turned, flung her arms around my neck, and said, "I don't know what I would have *done*, all these weeks, without you talking to me."

"Jewel," I protested. "I didn't do anything. You did it all yourself."

For a moment she looked startled. Then she put her mouth close to my ear and in a voice of unforgettable dignity said, "You let me talk. That's the same as talking to me."

I pulled back and looked at her. Her face seemed full of emotion. It was strained but alert, slightly puzzled but oddly excited. One thing it was not was exhausted.

19

Bobby's Salon

In college a classmate who thought my haircuts atrocious proposed taking me up to a hair-dressing establishment on Fifty-Seventh Street where she herself had been a customer since high school. "The place is a little odd," she said, "but this guy is terrific."

"Fifty-Seventh Street!" I protested.

"Don't worry about it," she said. "The address is Fifty-Seventh Street but the prices are Thirty-Fourth Street."

We climbed the stairs in a building directly across the street from Carnegie Hall, and on the third floor turned the knob on an unmarked door that led us into a large open space where a bank of windows looked out on the glamorous street, although they might just as well have been facing a street in Brooklyn or the Bronx, for all the relation the place seemed to have to Fifty-Seventh Street. The floor was covered in prison gray linoleum, the windows were heavily streaked, the walls needed a whitewash, and the furniture and fixtures—chairs, tables, lights, sink—all looked as though they'd been rescued from various coffee shop auctions. On the central window, in letters of shredded gilt, I read (backward, of course) the words, *Tony's Beauty Home.*

In the middle of the room, planted in an ancient barber chair, sat a woman with her neck swathed in a towel, getting her hair cut by a tall man with strong, handsome features and a thick shock of gray-black hair. Four or five women were sitting in these derelict chairs scattered around the room, reading or chatting. The man looked at me and my friend, and stopped cutting while the hand holding the scissors remained extended in the air; the other hand rested calmly on the woman's head looking, even from just inside the doorway, as though its touch would be as gentle as that of a doctor's on a patient's naked body.

"Hi, Florence," he said softly to my friend.

The women all looked up.

"I brought you a customer, Bobby," my friend said.

The man laughed and looked me over, as if trying to decide whether this was going to be a plus or a minus in his life. "Thanks," he said, in the same soft voice.

Everyone went back to reading and talking.

Florence and I sat down and the man with the scissors went back to work. As his scissors made contact with her hair, he said to the woman in the barber chair, "So, Laura, tell us about the scandal in City Hall. You work for that guy, don't you?"

One of the readers lowered her book and looked up expectantly.

"Yes, I do, but I can't talk about it," the woman in the chair said.

"Ah, c'mon, Laura," Bobby cajoled.

"Do you think he wrote the letter the cops found?" the reader asked.

"Of course he did," scoffed another woman.

"Oh, I wouldn't say 'of course' so quickly," said a third. "Once these things start unraveling they can turn out to be immensely complicated."

Meanwhile, the woman in the barber chair still refused to speak about the scandal to which she was supposedly privy, but she couldn't resist correcting the speculative remarks now loose in the room. As Bobby's eyes flew back and forth between the speakers, his scissors remained extended in the air for minutes at a time. I noticed that when he was following the rapid-fire verbal exchange of his customers, he didn't cut.

It was three o'clock in the afternoon. At six I walked out with the best haircut I had ever had. But was I grateful? "Do you realize we've been sitting there for three hours!" I fumed.

Florence shrugged. "It goes with the territory," she said. "The haircut's great, and you gotta put in the time to get it."

"You mean it's always like this?"

"Always."

"Why?"

"I can't really answer that question. I don't *know* why. It's just Bobby. He loves to keep his women waiting. Waiting and talking." She stopped short on the street. "It's the talking, I guess, that does it."

Bobby was Bobby Casella, a man in his sixties who'd been cutting hair in this room for more than forty years. He'd grown up in a tough Italian neighborhood in New Jersey where for as far back as he could remember, he had been an outcast because he announced regularly to the kids on the block that he was going to be an artist. "I didn't even know what an artist was," he'd tell you if you asked him about his growing-up years, "but, ya see, I knew I was *sensitive*, and I thought sensitive meant artist."

A lonely kid, he had loved visiting Tony-the-haircutter, a friend of the family who let Bobby watch while he worked. The sensitive misfit from New Jersey seemed to absorb the master's technique through his pores, and one day Tony invited him to cut *his* hair. Bobby was home free. No sooner were the scissors in his hand than he became the artist he had announced himself to be. He went to work for Tony in his twenties, and when Tony died Bobby simply stayed on, keeping the place as it was out of a superstition he called respect.

Bobby lived alone in a tiny apartment a few blocks from the shop, worked six days a week from early morning till late evening, and hated Sundays. One of the reasons he kept the customers waiting was that he himself never wanted to leave the place. For all intents and purposes, he was an isolate. His family had broken with him, he had no intimates, and only one or two acquaintances with whom he occasionally played handball but never met with off the courts. The truth was, he didn't know how to *be* in the world—I often thought he didn't even know that he was gay—and the shop was the only place where he occupied his skin with ease. Working meant not only the undying pleasure of cutting hair, it also meant inhaling a sense of world that he himself could create daily by keeping his women waiting—waiting and talking.

Although he held in reverence his own skill with the scissors, as the years went on he had come to long for an intensity that hair-cutting alone could not supply. Lively conversation, however, did often do the trick. When he had one of us in the chair—although I walked out grumbling that first day I, too, became one of Bobby's regulars—and could prod us into talking about ourselves in a way meant to provoke conversation, in no time you had sparks going, and Bobby's face became ecstatic. It didn't much matter what the subject was, or what was being argued, or even what the words themselves were actually saying. If the exchange grew heated, Bobby's voice would titter (Ooooh, what you just said!) and his hand would cover his mouth in mock horror, but his eyes shone and his sallow cheeks danced. Suddenly the shop was filled with the excitement of an exchange that sounded in his ears like drama: if it went on long enough it was like watching a play or reading a book. This was where the beauty lay for him: in the feeling that life—otherwise gray and empty—had become a story. When a conversation exhausted itself Bobby would invariably observe, his voice husky with happiness, "That was some story, wasn't it, girls."

How he got every one of us going was always something of a mystery, but his need was pressing and it made him shameless. No sooner had you become his customer than Bobby had taken your vital statistics—where you lived, what sort of work you did, who your husband was, whether you had a husband, and if not why not—and registered them on a rolodex in his mind that was invariably being consulted for an opening gambit, just as you were sinking into the tattered old barber chair. This bit of social manipulation coupled, somewhat eerily, with the gentleness of his touch, the crooning quality of his voice, the way his lips lingered on your cheek as he put the towel around your neck—all arts of seduction he practiced without restraint— almost always insured the conversational starter he craved.

"So, Stephanie," he would say, his voice liquid soft, as he was tying the knot in the towel, "tell us about your husband, the Nobel Prize winner."

Or, "Gloria, that job of yours as vice president with a major Wall Street firm. What is it again, that you do there?"

Or, "How's your new book doing, Vivian? The one on why women don't trust men. Someone told me she saw a not so good review in *Time* magazine."

Every one of us, whether we reacted with amusement ("Bobby, what kind of a question is that to ask?") or exasperation ("For God's sake, Bobby, stop it!"), was cajoled into responding. I was one of those who were usually exasperated—his insinuating style got under my skin— nonetheless I always gave him *something*. It wasn't just that I wanted the haircuts badly enough to grant Bobby's terms, I, like every one of his customers, had become hooked on the place.

The women in the room ran the kind of New York gamut that Central Casting might have supplied. On any given day, you'd have sitting in those chairs a Republican committee woman, a Lincoln Center dancer, an Upper West Side activist, someone in banking or business, and, of course, a social worker, a therapist, a teacher. We ranged in age from twenty-five to eighty; we dressed in everything from Bergdorf's to thrift shops; we read Proust, the *Wall Street Journal*, self-help books, and the *New Yorker*.

When I think back on those long afternoons at Bobby's, I see how reflective they were, decade by decade, at any given moment, of the single element that unified us. The conversation might range from electoral politics to city life versus suburban living to the newest novel to whether the Japanese got more heart attacks than Americans—but, ultimately, what made it come into vivid focus was the question of how men saw it, as opposed to how women saw it. This, finally, was the frame of reference from which— with savvy, shrewdness, and vitality—nearly all questions were considered. A situation would be posed, personal testimony given, and while the responses, intellectually speaking, ranged far and wide, it was the interjected commentary on our life with men that was most memorable: "How interesting, he said that, and you didn't leave him" or "O-mi-gahd, isn't that rho-maaan-tic" or "It's as though he never hears a word I say" (this last especially was a favorite). Then, almost invariably, the talk would take a dive as someone holding the *New Yorker* in her lap sighed "Thus it ever was, thus it will ever be" with some smartly dressed woman in her fifties rattling the pages of the *Times* while she pronounced, "Forget it, they're all a bunch of shits. You don't reason with them, you isolate them in a laboratory."

Regardless of what was said about men during these years, Bobby—as though he himself bore no relation to the species—was enraptured. His eyes would glow, his mouth grin, and his head bob back and forth among the speakers, as though he'd become a witness to some great spectator sport that only the privileged were privy to.

In my thirties, the script began to change. The women's movement had now declared the personal political, and the conversation at *Tony's Beauty Home* was beginning to take notice. The new talk of women's rights induced highly opinionated response as usual, only now the anecdotal evidence often triggered theoretical speculation instead of sit-com conclusions. There was still always someone moaning, "O-mi-gahd, that's so rho-maaan-tic" but the knee-jerk "thus it ever was" no longer had the final word.

Bobby's scissors would stop in midair for minutes at a time as he listened, mesmerized, to some position paper being delivered by a young woman in jeans with *Sisterhood Is Powerful* in her lap while the Republican committee woman opened her mouth two or three times but somehow failed to speak. Now it was cultural history that was in the dock, not simply men. How exhilarating the woman in jeans made it sound! It was centuries of sexism that was guilty, not "men as such." I remember she was forever saying "men as such." If I was in the chair while she was orating, Bobby would whisper excitedly into my ear, "Is she right, is she right?"

By the late '80s we were all familiar with the charge against cultural history, and keenly aware that its implied revolution had not exactly been accomplished; especially not on the third floor across the street from Carnegie Hall. Yet, in an oddly telling way, the atmosphere in Bobby's shop reflected the strong discomfort of this provocative juncture. Conversations that seemed to be going down a familiar road would suddenly veer off in an unexpected direction, take a startling turn, drop into a cul-de-sac: developments that inevitably reminded one of the changing but not yet changed times; or, put another way, of times that often looked as if they were as they had always been, but in fact were not. Bobby went on loving it all indiscriminately: his eyes sparkling, his mouth giggling, his lips caressing the cheek of the woman in the chair as he breathed into her ear, "That was some story, wasn't it?" Never noticing how often she now turned around to stare at him with puzzlement in her eyes.

One day during this period I took a seat in the shop while a woman with a mass of gray-brown hair sat in the barber chair, talking about how impossible her daughter was becoming, she just didn't know *what* the girl wanted. To my left sat the woman reading the *Times* (there was always at least one), to my right a woman with a pop psychology paperback on her lap, and farther down the row, two others looking quietly off into space. One of these was a woman in her seventies, beautifully dressed, her hair strikingly thick and white, her skin soft and remarkably unwrinkled. She was the next one to take her place in the chair. When she did, I saw her eyes. They were bright blue and they were cold, very cold: sunlight on winter water.

Bobby smoothed back her hair with a tenderness born of long familiarity.

"How are ya, Rose?" he said softly, his lips close to her ear.

"Oh, Bobby, for God's sake!" she said sharply, pushing his face away.

"Same old Rose," he laughed.

Her lips narrowed and she shrugged one shoulder.

Bobby began to cut her hair.

For a little the room was silent; but for how long could Bobby sustain silence?

"So tell us about your marriage, Rose," he said.

Two of us looked up, startled.

"For God's sake, Bobby," the woman in the chair said, "I will *not*."

"Aw, c'mon, Rose, everybody would love to hear about your marriage."

The *Times* reader looked over the top of her paper.

"It's a very romantic story," Bobby said.

"You've heard it a thousand times," Rose sniffed.

"Yeah, but *they* haven't."

"What am I? A performing animal? I have to tell that story every time I come here? *Please.*"

"Ah-h-h, don't be that way, Rose," Bobby pleaded, his hands cupping her head.

"Just cut, Bobby, okay?"

"Ah-h-h, Rose, don't be that way," he said again, his voice now a liquid sedative.

The woman in the chair shrugged, but clearly the fight had gone out of her.

"Well, as you know," she said, bringing her fingertips together over her lap, her head now inclining toward Bobby,

"I was living in the Bronx at that time. When I first met him. Working in Manhattan, but living in the Bronx." Her eyes landed on the woman with the pop psychology book who was now looking up. "In those days there weren't so many of us who went to business, you know," Rose said to this woman. "This is fifty years ago we're talking about.

"So if you wanted to stay respectable, and of course I did, you lived with a family. Either in the Bronx or in Brooklyn. I would have lived in Brooklyn with my sister but my brother-in-law wouldn't have me in the house. He said I turned her against him. All I did was give her another pair of eyes to see what any child could see, how rotten he was, but that's another story. So I went to live with this very nice family in the Bronx, where I had a room and a toilet all to myself and the subway two blocks away. In fact, mine was the last stop on the line so every morning I sat five or ten minutes in the train, waiting for it to start, enjoying my paper.

"One day I see a nice-looking gentleman is sitting across from me, reading the same paper, and he's smiling at the same story I'm smiling at. The next day he's there again, again across from me, again reading the paper. This goes on for a good few weeks. One morning I look up, and he nods at me. I'm a little startled but I nod back, after all, we're human beings, aren't we, and after that, every morning he sits across from me, and we nod at each other. *This* goes on for a good few weeks, maybe even months. Then he comes across the aisle, points at the seat next to me, and says, 'May I?' Well, by this time, it would have been funny for me to say no, right? So I said, 'It's a free country. Be my guest.'"

With those words Rose fell silent. The woman with the *Times* started reading again.

"Yeah, Rose?" Bobby prompted. "What happened then?"

"What happened then," she said dismissively. "What do you think happened then. We began to talk. Every morning after that we talked for the entire hour it took us to get to Forty-Second Street, which is where I got off. He went one stop further to Thirty-Fourth. We talked and talked and talked. I can hardly believe it now, when I look back on it, how much we had to say to each other! So, as you can imagine, one thing led to another. And one day he asks me if we can have dinner together some time.

"I told him straight out, then and there, it could never be. 'Mr. Levinson,' I said, 'you are a married man and I am a respectable girl.'"

"What!" the woman in jeans ejaculated. "He was *married*?"

"Yes. Didn't I tell you that? Max Levinson was a married man."

This time everyone looked up.

Again Rose paused, again Bobby prompted her.

"So what happened then, Rose? What did you do after that?"

"What did I do after that. Nothing. I did exactly nothing. We continued as we were. Except that every day now he begged me to meet him after work. Or even during the lunch hour. I wouldn't do it. For months and months I wouldn't do it. But he was at me constantly. He wore me down like water on a stone. One day I agreed. Lunch. After that, I have to admit, I got a little weaker. We began to meet almost every day for lunch, and I let him take my arm crossing the street. And I have to say I began to get used to it, and I liked it, I liked it very much. Whether or not I liked *him*, I don't know, but I liked *it*, if you know what I mean."

The women in the room nodded as one.

"So then what, Rose? Then what?"

"So then we went on like *that* for a few months. By now, time is passing. It's more than a couple of years already that I know Max Levinson. And he's at me all the time to go with him, if you know what I mean. God, how that man hounded me. So I tell him, if you want me, Max, you gotta leave Mrs. Levinson. This, he tells me, he cannot do. Why? She is a very sick woman, he couldn't live with himself if he left her. So, alright, I say, in that case there is nothing to be done. We have a situation we cannot solve. But still, he wants what he wants. He cannot give me up, he says. He loves me with a love he has never felt before, he says. Have me he must, he says."

"O-mi-gahd, it's so romantic," breathed the fourth woman in the room.

She had us all now.

"So then what, Rose?" Bobby pleaded.

"So I determine I must leave the place I am living, and go to live somewhere else where he will not see me anymore. And that is what I did. One day I got myself a room in another neighborhood, on another subway line, and I just disappeared. Max called the house a million times. He drove that family crazy. But I had left strict orders to tell him nothing, absolutely nothing. I was gone from his life."

The room was silent.

"Yes, Rose? Then what, Rose?"

"Five years passed. I never saw him, he never saw me. What had happened to each of us, nobody knew. Then, one Sunday I'm walking with my girlfriend in the street, in Greenwich Village, of all places, and suddenly there is Max Levinson in front of me. He takes me by the arm, asks my girlfriend to kindly go home, and marches me off to a restaurant. He sits down with a cup of coffee and a piece of Danish, and he tells me he's never stopped thinking of me, not in all these years, and he begs me not to disappear again.

"So it started all over again: walks, talks, lunches, and again he's begging me to go with him. I tell him I'm willing to meet him for a meal and a walk, but I'm still respectable and I will not go with him. In this way a year goes by. Then one day he calls me and he says, 'Guess what?' 'What?' I say. 'She's dead,' he says. 'She died last night.'

You could have heard a feather drop on the prison gray linoleum.

"So then what, Rose?" Bobby breathed into her ear.

"Then what," she shrugged. "What do you think, then what. We got married."

Period. End of story. Rose shut her mouth as if this time she really meant to keep it shut. Bobby was grinning from ear to ear, his eyes bright, his head shaking itself in wonder—what a story, what a story—he couldn't wait for the conversation to begin. He hardly noticed that the atmosphere in the room had grown tense; or that the silence had persisted. At last it was I, urged on by the irreverent times, who spoke.

"So how was it, Rose?" I asked.

Her lips compressed themselves into a thin line and she stared off into the middle distance. A minute went by; then another; then she spoke.

"I don't regret it," she said firmly.

Again: not a sound in the room.

"That bad, eh?" I said.

She turned fully toward me and I saw that the sun had gone down on the blue of her eyes. They were no longer cold, nor did they glitter. A flat, vacant calm had relieved them of all expression.

"He was a man," she said, "he heard the sound of no voice but his own."

We all stared at the floor.

"That's some story, isn't it, girls?" Bobby giggled nervously.

I looked up and saw the confusion in his face. Everyone had always laughed out loud at Rose's recital—it was one of the great Battle of the Sexes stories—why weren't they laughing now? Very quickly, confusion morphed into alarm. For the first time since I'd been coming here Bobby put down his scissors while a woman was still in the chair. Right then and there I saw his life change: the comedy of women and men together had begun to die in him. Even he knew that more than an era had completed itself in *Tony's Beauty Home*.

ESSAYS IN FEMINISM

20

Consciousness

In a lower Manhattan office a legal secretary returns from her lunch hour, sinks into her seat, and says miserably to a secretary at the next desk, "I don't know what's happening to me. A perfectly nice construction worker whistled and said, 'My, isn't *that* nice,' as I passed him, and suddenly I felt this terrific anger pushing up in me . . . I swear I wanted to *hit* him!"

At the same time, a thoughtful forty-year-old mother in a Maryland suburb is saying to a visiting relative over early-afternoon coffee, "You know, I've been thinking lately, I'm every bit as smart as Harry, and yet he got the Ph.D. and I raised the girls. Mind you, I *wanted* to stay home. And yet, the thought of my two girls growing up and doing the same thing doesn't sit well with me at all. Not at all."

And in Toledo, Ohio, a factory worker turns to the next woman on the inspection belt and confides, "Last night I told Jim, 'I been working in the same factory as you ten years now. We go in at the same time, come out at the same time. But I do all the shopping, get the dinner, wash the dishes, and on Sunday break my back down on the kitchen floor. I'm real tired of doin' all that. I want some help from you.' Well, he just laughed at me, see? Like he done every time I mentioned this before. But last night I wouldn't let up. I mean, I really *meant* it this time. And you know? I thought he was gonna let me have it. Looked mighty like he was gettin' ready to belt me one. But you know? I just didn't care! I wasn't gonna back down, come hell or high water. You'll just never believe it, he'd kill me if he knew I was tellin' you, he washed the dishes. First time in his entire life."

None of these women are feminists. None of them are members of the women's liberation movement. None of them ever heard of consciousness raising. And yet, each of them exhibits the symptomatic influences of this, the movement's most esoteric practice. Each of them, without specific awareness, is beginning to feel the effects of the consideration of woman's personal experience in a new light—a political light. Each of them is undergoing the mysterious behavioral twitches that indicate psychological alteration. Each of them is drawing on a linking network of feminist analysis and emotional upchucking that is beginning to suffuse the political-social air of American life today. Each of them, without ever having attended a consciousness-raising session, has had her consciousness raised.

Consciousness raising is the name given to the feminist practice of examining one's personal experience in the light of sexism—that theory which explains woman's subordinate position in society as a result of a cultural decision to confer direct power on men and only indirect power on women. The term of description and the practice to which it refers are derived from a number of sources—psychoanalysis, Marxist theory, and American revivalism, mainly—and was born out of the earliest stages of feminist formulation begun about three years ago in such predictable liberationist nesting places as Cambridge, New York, Chicago, and Berkeley. (The organization most prominently associated with the growth of consciousness raising is the New York Redstockings.)

Perceiving, first, that woman's position in our society does indeed constitute that of a political class, and, second, that woman's "natural" domain is her feelings, and, third, that testifying in a friendly and supportive atmosphere enables people to see that their experiences are often duplicated (thereby reducing their sense of isolation and increasing the desire to theorize as well as to confess), the radical feminists sensed quickly that a group of women sitting in a circle discussing their emotional experiences as though they were material for cultural analysis was political dynamite. Hence, through personal testimony and emotional analysis could the class consciousness of *women* be raised. And thus the idea of the small "women's group"—or consciousness-raising group—was delivered into a cruel but exciting world.

Consciousness raising is, at one and the same time, both the most celebrated and the most accessible introduction to the women's movement and the most powerful technique for feminist conversion known to the liberationists. Women are *drawn* to the practice out of a variety of discontents, but it's under the spell of a wholly new interpretation of their experience that they *remain*.

Coming together, as they do, week after week for many months, the women who are in a group begin to experience an extraordinary sense of commonality that is encouraged by the technique's instruction to look for explanations for each part of one's personal history in terms of the social or cultural dynamic created by sexism—rather than in terms of the individual dynamic, as one would ordinarily do in group therapy. Although there are many differences between consciousness raising and group therapy—for example, the former involves no professional leader, no exchange of money—the fundamental difference lies in this fact: in consciousness raising one looks not to one's unique emotional history for an explanation of behavioral problems but rather to the cultural fact of the patriarchy.

Thus, looking at one's history and experience in consciousness-raising sessions is rather like shaking a kaleidoscope and watching all the same pieces rearrange themselves into an altogether *other* picture, one that suddenly makes the color and shape of each piece appear startlingly new and alive, and full of unexpected meaning. (This is mainly why feminists often say that women are the most interesting people around these days, because they are experiencing the psychic invigoration of self-rediscovery.)

What *does* take place in a consciousness-raising group? How *do* the women see themselves? What *is* the thrust of the conversation at a typical session? Is it simply the venting of man-hating spleen that is caricatured by the unsympathetic press? Or the unfocused and wrongheaded theorizing insisted upon by the insulated intellectuals? Or yet again, the self-indulgent navel-gazing that many tight-lipped leftie activists see it as?

"In this room," says Roberta H., a Long Island housewife speaking euphemistically of her group's meetings, "we do not generalize. We do not speak of any experience except that of the women here. We follow the rules for consciousness raising as set out by the New York Radical Feminists and we do not apply them to 'woman's experience'— whatever on earth that is—we apply them to ourselves. But, oh God! The samenesses we have found, and the way in which these meetings have changed our lives!"

The rules that Roberta H. is referring to are to be found in a mimeographed pamphlet, an introduction to the New York Radical Feminists organization, which explains the purpose and procedures of consciousness raising. The sessions consist mainly of women gathering once a week, sitting in a circle and speaking in turn, addressing themselves—almost entirely out of personal experience—to a topic that has been preselected. The pamphlet sets forth the natural limits of a group (ten to fifteen women), advises women to start a group from among their friends and on a word-of-mouth basis, and suggests a list of useful topics for discussion. These topics include Love, Marriage, Sex, Work, Femininity, How I Came to Women's Liberation, Motherhood, Aging, and Competition with Other Women. Additional subjects are developed as a particular group's specific interests and circumstances begin to surface.

When a group's discussions start to revolve more and more about apparently very individual circumstances, they often lead to startling similarities. For instance, a Westchester County group composed solely of housewives, who felt that each marriage represented a unique meaning in each of their lives, used the question, "Why did you marry the man you married?" as the subject for discussion one night. "We went around the room," says Joan S., one of the women present, "and while some of us seemed unable to answer that question without going back practically to the cradle, do you know?, the word love was never mentioned *once.*"

On the Upper West Side of Manhattan, in the vicinity of Columbia University, a group of women between the ages of thirty-five and forty-five have been meeting regularly for six months. Emily R., an attractive forty-year-old divorcée in this group, says: "When I walked into the first meeting, and saw the *types* there, I said to myself: 'None of these broads have been through what I've been through. They couldn't possibly feel the way I feel.' Well, I'll tell you. None of them *have* been through what I've been through if you look at our experience superficially. But when you look a little *deeper*—the way we've been doing at these meetings— you see they've *all* been through what I've been through, and they all feel pretty much the way I feel. God, when I saw *that!* When I saw that what I always felt was my own personal hang-up was as true for every other woman in that room as it was for me! Well, that's when *my* consciousness was raised."

What Emily R. speaks of is the phenomenon most often referred to in the movement, the flash of insight most directly responsible for the feminist leap in faith being made by hundreds of women everywhere—the intensely felt realization that what had always been taken for symptoms of personal unhappiness or dissatisfaction or frustration was so powerfully and so consistently duplicated among women that perhaps these symptoms could just as well be ascribed to *cultural* causes as to psychological ones.

In the feminist movement this kind of "breakthrough" can occur nowhere else but in a consciousness-raising group. It is only here, during many months of meetings, that a woman is able finally—if ever—to bring to the surface those tangled feelings of anger, bafflement, and frustrated justice that have drawn her to the movement in the first place. It is only here that the dynamic of sexism will finally strike home, finally make itself felt in the living detail of her own life.

Claire K., a feminist activist in Cambridge, says of women's groups: "I've been working with women's groups for over two years now. The average life of a group is a year to eighteen months, and believe me, I've watched a lot of them fold before they ever got off the ground. But, when they *work!* There is a rhythm to some of them that's like life itself. You watch a group expand and contract, and each time it does one or the other it never comes back together quite the same. Something happens to the women and to the group itself. Each time, if they survive, they have *grown*. You can see it, almost smell it and taste it."

I am one of those feminists who are always mourning after the coherent and high-minded leadership of the nineteenth-century women's movement. Often, when I observe the fragmented, intellectually uneven, politically disparate components of the women's movement today, I experience dismay, and I find myself enviously imagining Elizabeth Cady Stanton and Lucretia Mott and Susan B. Anthony holding hands, so to speak, for forty years, performing an act of mutual sustenance that gave interwoven shape to their lives and their cause. And I think in a panic, Where would we be without them? They thought it all out for us, and we've got not one inch beyond them. Lately, however, I have changed my mind about that . . .

I was on my way to a meeting one night not too long ago, a meeting meant to fashion a coalition group out of the movement's many organizations. I knew exactly what was ahead of me. I knew that a woman from NOW (National Organization of Women) would rise and speak about our "image"; that a Third Worlder would announce loudly she didn't give a good goddamn about anybody's orgasms, her women were starving, for chrissake; that a Radicalesbian would insist that the women's movement must face the problem of sexism from within *right now*; and ten women from the Socialist Workers Party would walk out to protest against middle-class "elitist" control in the movement. I knew there would be a great deal of emotional opinion delivered, a comparatively small amount of valuable observation made, and some action taken. Suddenly, as the bus I was on swung westward through Central Park, I realized that it didn't matter, that none of it mattered. I realized it was stupid and self-pitying to be wishing that the meeting was going to be chaired by Elizabeth Stanton. She had worked and spoken—profoundly—in the idiom of her time, and while in my time no woman in the movement was her equal, something else was: the consciousness-raising group.

I saw then that the small anonymous consciousness-raising group was the heart and soul of the women's movement, that it is not what happens at movement meetings in New York or Boston or Berkeley that counts but the fact that hundreds of these groups are springing up daily—at universities in Kansas, in small towns in Oregon, in the suburbs of Detroit—out of a responsiveness urged into existence by modern radical feminism. It is here that a new psychology of the self—a political psychology—is being forged. The consciousness-raising group of today is the true second front of feminism. The ghost of Susan B. began hovering over me, nodding vigorously, "Well done, my dear, well done."

That ghost has accompanied me to every movement meeting I have attended since that night, but when I am at a consciousness-raising session she disappears and I am on my own. Then, for better or worse, I am the full occupant of my feminist skin, engaged in the true business of modern feminism, reaching hard for self-possession.

And now let's go to a consciousness-raising session.

Early in the evening, on a crisp autumn night, a young woman in an apartment in the Gramercy Park section of Manhattan signs a letter, puts it in an envelope, turns out the light over her desk, gets her coat out of the hall closet, runs down two flights of stairs, hails a taxi, and heads west directly across the city. At the same time, on the Upper West Side, another woman, slightly older than the first, bends over a sleeping child, kisses his forehead, says goodnight to the babysitter, rides down twelve flights in an elevator, walks over to Broadway, and disappears into the downtown subway. Across town, on the Upper East Side, another woman tosses back a head of stylishly fixed hair, pulls on a beautiful pair of suede boots, and leaves her tiny apartment, also heading down and across town. On the Lower East Side, in a fourth-floor tenement apartment, a woman five or six years younger than all the others combs out a tangled mop of black hair, clomps down the stairs in her Swedish clogs, and starts trudging west on St. Marks Place. In a number of other places all over Manhattan other women are also leaving their houses. When the last one finally walks into the Greenwich Village living room they are all headed for, there are ten women in the room.

These women range in age from the late twenties to the middle thirties; in appearance, from attractive to very beautiful; in education, from bachelor's degrees to master's degrees; in marital status, from single to married to divorced to imminently separated; two are mothers. Their names are Veronica, Lucie, Diana, Marie, Laura, Jen, Sheila, Dolores, Marilyn, and Claire. Their occupations, respectively, are assistant television producer, graduate student, housewife, copywriter, journalist, unemployed actress, legal secretary, unemployed college graduate, schoolteacher, and computer programmer.

They are not movement women; neither are they committed feminists; nor are they marked by a special sense of social development or by personal neurosis. They are simply a rather ordinary group of women who are drawn out of some unresolved, barely articulated need to form a "women's group." They are in their third month of meetings; they are now at Marie's house (next week they will meet at Laura's, and after that at Jen's, and so on down the line); the subject for discussion tonight is "Work."

The room is large, softly lit, comfortably furnished. After ten or fifteen minutes of laughing, chatting, note and book exchanging, the women arrange themselves in a circle, some on chairs, some on the couch, others on the floor. In the center of the circle is a low coffee table covered with a coffeepot, cups, sugar, milk, plates of cheese and bread, cookies and fruit. Marie suggests they begin, and turning to the woman on her right, who happens to be Dolores, asks if she would be the first.

DOLORES (*the unemployed college graduate*): I guess that's okay . . . I'd just as soon be the first . . . mainly because I hate to be the last. When I'm last, all I think about is, soon it will be my turn. (*She looks up nervously.*) You've no idea how I *hate* talking in public. (*There is a long pause; silence in the circle.*) . . . Work! God, what can I say? The whole question has always been absolute hell for me . . . A lot of you have said your fathers ignored you when you were growing up and paid attention only to your brothers. Well, in my house it was just the opposite. I have two sisters, and my father always told me I was the smartest of all, that I was smarter than he was, and that I could do anything I wanted to do . . . but somehow, I don't really know why, everything I turned to came to nothing. After six years in analysis I still don't know why. (*She looks off into space for a moment and her eyes seem to lose the train of her*

thought. Then she shakes herself and goes on.) I've always
drifted . . . just drifted. My parents never forced me to work.
I needn't work even now. I had every opportunity to find
out what I really wanted to do. But . . . nothing I did satisfied me, and I would just stop . . . Or turn away . . . Or go
on a trip. I worked for a big company for a while . . . Then
my parents went to Paris and I just went with them . . . I
came back . . . I went to school . . . I was a researcher at
Time-Life . . . drifted . . . got   married . . . divorced . . .
drifted. (*Her voice grows more halting.*) I feel my life is such
waste. I'd like to write, I really would; I feel I'd be a good
writer, but I don't know. I just can't get going . . . My father
is so disappointed in me. He keeps hoping I'll really do
something. Soon. (*She shrugs her shoulders but her face is
very quiet and pale, and her pain expressive. She happens to be
one of the most beautiful women in the room.*)

DIANA (*the housewife*): What do you think you will do?
DOLORES (*in a defiant burst*): Try to get married!
JEN (*the unemployed actress*) and MARIE (*the copy-
writer*): Oh no!

CLAIRE (*the computer programmer*): After all that!
Haven't you learned yet? What on earth is marriage going
to do for you? Who on earth could you marry? Feeling
about yourself as you do? Who could save you from
yourself? Because that's what you want.

MARILYN (*the schoolteacher*): That's right. It sounds
like "It's just all too much to think out so I might as well
get married."

LUCIE (*the graduate student*): Getting married like that
is bound to be a disaster.

JEN: And when you get married like that it's always to some creep you've convinced yourself is wonderful. So understanding. (*Dolores grows very red and very quiet through all this.*)

SHEILA (*the legal secretary*): Stop jumping on her like that! I know *just* how she feels . . . I was *really* raised to be a wife and a mother, and yet my father wanted me to do something with my education after he sent me to one of the best girls' schools in the East. Well, I didn't get married when I got out of school like half the girls I graduated with, and now seven years later I'm *still* not married. (*She stops talking abruptly and looks off into the space in the center of the circle, her attention wandering as though she's suddenly lost her way.*) I don't know how to describe it exactly, but I know just how Dolores feels about drifting. I've always worked, and yet something was always sort of confused inside me. I never really knew which way I wanted to go on a job: up, down, sideways . . . I always thought it would be the most marvelous thing in the world to work for a really brilliant and important man. I never have. But I've worked for some good men and I've learned a lot from them. But (*her dark head comes up two or three inches and she looks hesitantly around*) I don't know about the rest of you, but I've always wound up being proposi-tioned by my bosses. It's a funny thing. As soon as I'd be doing really well, learning fast and taking on some genuine responsibility, like it would begin to excite them, and they'd make their move. When I refused, almost invariably they'd begin to *browbeat* me. I mean, they'd make my life miserable! And, of course, I'd retreat . . . I'd get small and scared and take everything they were dishing out . . . and then I'd move on. I don't know, maybe something in my behavior was really asking for it, I honestly don't know anymore.

MARIE: There's a good chance you *were* asking for it. I work with a lot of men and I don't get propositioned every other day. I am so absolutely straight no one *dares* . . . They all think I am a dyke.

SHEILA (*plaintively*): Why is it like that, though? Why are men like that? Is it something they have more of, this sexual need for ego gratification? Are they made differently from us?

JEN (*placing her coffee cup on the floor beside her*): No! You've just never learned to stand up for yourself! And goddammit, they *know* it, and they play on it. Look, you all know I've been an actress for years. Well, once, when I was pretty new in the business, I was playing opposite this guy. He used to feel me up on the stage. All the *time.* I was scared. I didn't know what to do. I'd say to the stage manager: That guy is feeling me up. The stage manager would look at me like I was crazy, and shrug his shoulders. Like: What can *I* do? Well, once I finally thought: I can't stand this. And I bit him. Yes, I bit the bastard, I bit his tongue while he was kissing me.

A CHORUS OF VOICES: You bit him????

JEN (*with great dignity*): Yes, dammit, I bit him. And afterward he said to me, "Why the hell did you do that?" And I said, "You know goddamn well why I did that." And do you know? He respected me after that. (*She laughs.*) Didn't like me very much. But he respected me. (*She looks distracted for a moment.*) . . . I guess that *is* pretty funny. I mean, biting someone's tongue during a love scene.

VERONICA (*the assistant TV producer*): Yeah. Very funny.

LAURA (*the journalist*): Listen, I've been thinking about something Sheila said. That as soon as she began to get really good at her job her boss would make a pass—and that would pretty much signal the end, right? She'd refuse, he'd become an S.O.B., and she'd eventually leave. It's almost as if sex were being used to cut her down, or back, or in some way stop her from rising. An *instinct* he, the boss, has—to sleep with her when he feels her becoming really independent.

LUCIE (*excitedly*): I'll buy that! Look, it's like Samson and Delilah in reverse. *She* knew that sex would give her the opportunity to destroy his strength. Women are famous for wanting to sleep with men in order to enslave them, right? That's the great myth, right? He's all spirit and mind, she's all emotion and biological instinct. She uses this instinct with *cunning* to even out the score, to get some power, to bring him down—through sex. But look at it another way. What are these guys always saying to us? What are they always saying about women's liberation?—"All she needs is a good fuck." They say that *hopefully. Prayerfully.* They know. We all know what all that "All she needs is a good fuck" stuff is all about.

CLAIRE: This is ridiculous. Use your heads. Isn't a guy kind of super if he wants to sleep with a woman who's becoming independent?

MARIE: Yes, but not in business. There's something wrong every time, whenever sex is operating in business. It's always like a secret weapon, something you hit your opponent below the belt with.

DIANA: God, you're all crazy! Sex is *fun*. Wherever it exists. It's warm and nice and it makes people feel good.

DOLORES: That's a favorite pipedream of yours, isn't it?

SHEILA: It certainly doesn't seem like very much fun to me when I watch some secretary coming on to one of the lawyers when she wants a raise, then I see the expression on her face as she turns away.

MARIE: God, that sounds like my mother when she wants something from my father!

VERONICA (*feebly*): You people are beginning to make me feel awful! (*Everyone's head snaps in her direction.*)

MARIE: Why?

VERONICA: The way you're talking about using sex at work. As if it were so horrible. Well, I've *always* used a kind of sexy funniness to get what I want at work. What's wrong with that?

LUCIE: What do you do?

VERONICA: Well, if someone is being very stuffy and serious about business, I'll say something funny—I guess in a sexy way to break up the atmosphere, which sometimes gets so heavy. You know what I mean? Men can be so pretentious in business! And then, usually, I get what I want—while I'm being funny and cute, and they're laughing.

DIANA (*heatedly*): Look, don't you see what you're doing?

VERONICA (*testily*): No, I don't. What am I doing?

DIANA (*her hands moving agitatedly through the air before her*): If there's some serious business going on you come in and say: Nothing to be afraid of, folks. Just frivolous, feminine little me. I'll tell a joke, wink my eye, do a little dance, and we'll all pretend nothing's really happening here.

VERONICA: My God, I never thought of it like that.

LAURA: It's like those apes. They did a study of apes in which they discovered that apes chatter and laugh and smile a lot to ward off aggression.

MARILYN: Just like women! Christ, aren't they always saying to us: *Smile!* Who tells a man to smile? And how often do you smile for no damned reason, right? It's so *natural* to start smiling as soon as you start talking to a man, isn't it?

LUCIE: That's right! You're right! You know—God, it's amazing!—I began to think about this just the other day. I was walking down Fifth Avenue and a man in the doorway of a store said to me, "Whatsamatta, honey? Things can't be *that* bad." And I was startled because I wasn't feeling depressed or anything, and I couldn't figure out why he was saying that. So I looked, real fast, in the glass to see what my face looked like. And it didn't look like anything. It was just a face at rest. I had just an ordinary, sort of thoughtful expression on my face. And he thought I was *depressed*. And I couldn't help it, I said to myself, Would he have said that to you if you were a man? And I answered myself immediately: No!

DIANA: That's it. That's really what they want. To keep us barefoot, pregnant, and *smiling*. Always sort of begging, you know? Just a little supplicating—at all times. And they get anxious if you stop smiling. Not because you're depressed. Because you're *thinking*!

DOLORES: Oh, come on now. Surely, there are lots of men who have very similar kinds of manners? What about all the life-of-the-party types? All those clowns and regular guys?

CLAIRE: Yes, what about them? You never take those guys seriously. You never think of the men of real power, the guys with serious intentions and real strength, acting that way, do you? And those are the ones with real responsibility. The others are the ones women laugh about in private, the ones who become our confidants, not our lovers, the ones who are *just like ourselves*.

SHEILA (*quietly*): You're right.

LUCIE: And it's true, it really does undercut your seriousness, all that smiling.

SHEILA (*looking suddenly sad and very intent*): And underscore your weakness.

DOLORES: Yes, exactly. We smile because we feel at a loss, because we feel vulnerable. We don't quite know how to accomplish what we want to accomplish or how to navigate through life, so we act *feminine*. That's really what this is all about, isn't it? To be masculine is to take action, to be feminine is to smile. Be coy and cute and sexy—and maybe you'll become the big man's assistant. God, it's all so sad . . .

VERONICA (*looking a bit dazed*): I never thought of any of it like this. But it's true, I guess, all of it. You know (*and now her words come in a rush and her voice grows stronger*). I've always been afraid of my job. I've always felt I was there by *accident*, and that any minute they were gonna find me out. Any minute, they'd know I was a fraud. I had the chance to become a producer recently, and I fudged it. I didn't realize for two weeks afterward that I'd done it deliberately, that I don't *want* to move up, that I'm afraid of the responsibility, that I'd rather stay where I am, making my little jokes and not drawing attention to myself . . .

(*Veronica's voice fades away, but her face seems full of struggle, and for a long moment no one speaks.*)

MARILYN (*her legs pulled up under her on the couch, running her hand distractedly through her short blond hair*): Lord, does *that* sound familiar! Do I know that feeling of being there by accident, any minute here comes the axe. I've never felt that anything I got—any honor, any prize, any decent job—was really legitimately mine. I always felt it was luck, that I happened to be in the right place at the right time and that I was able to put up a good front and people just didn't know . . . but if I stuck around long enough they would . . . So, I guess I've drifted a lot, too. Being married, I took advantage of it. I remember when my husband was urging me to work, telling me I was a talented girl and that I shouldn't just be sitting around the house taking care of the baby. I wanted so to be persuaded by him, but I just couldn't do it. Every night I'd say, "Tomorrow's the day," and every morning I'd get up feeling like my head was full of molasses, so sluggish I couldn't *move*. By the time I'd finally get out of that damn bed it was too late to get a babysitter or too late to get to a job interview or too late to do anything, really. (*She turns toward Diana.*) You're a housewife, Diana. You must know what I mean. (*Diana nods ruefully.*) I began concentrating on my sex life with my husband, which had never been any too good, and was now getting really bad. It's hard to explain. We'd always been very affectionate with one another, and we still were. But I began to crave . . . passion. (*She smiles: almost apologetically.*) What else can I call it? There was no passion between us, practically no intercourse. I began to *demand* it. My husband reacted very badly, accused me of—oh God, the most awful things! Then I had an affair. The sex was great, the man was very tender with me for a long while. I felt *revived*. But then, a funny thing happened. I became almost hypnotized by the sex. I couldn't get enough, I couldn't stop thinking about it, it seemed to consume me; and yet, I became as sluggish now with sexual desire as I had been when I couldn't get up to look for a job. Sometimes, I felt so sluggish I could hardly prepare myself to go meet my lover. And then . . . (*She stops talking and looks down at the floor. Her forehead is creased, her brows draw together, she seems pierced suddenly by memory. Everyone remains quiet for a long moment.*)

DIANA (*very gently*): And then?

MARILYN (*almost shaking herself awake*): And then the man told my husband of our affair.

JEN: Oh Christ!

MARILYN: My husband went wild . . . (*Her voice trails off and again everyone remains silent, this time until she speaks again.*) He left me. We've been separated a year and a half now. So then I *had* to go to work. And I have, I have. But it remains a difficult, difficult thing. I do the most ordinary kind of work, afraid to strike out, afraid to try anything that involves real risk. It's almost as if there's some *training* necessary for taking risks, and I just don't have it . . . and my husband leaving me, and forcing me out to work, somehow didn't magically give me whatever it takes to get that training.

LAURA (*harshly*): Maybe it's too late.

DIANA: Well, that's a helluva thought. (*She crosses her legs and stares at the floor. Everyone looks toward her, but she says no more. Jen stretches, Claire bites into a cookie, Lucie pours coffee, and everyone rearranges themselves in their seats.*)

MARIE (*after a long pause*): It's your turn, Diana.

DIANA (*turning in her chair and running thin hands nervously through her curly red hair*): It's been hard for me to concentrate on the subject. I went to see my mother in the hospital this afternoon, and I haven't been able to stop thinking about her all day long.

JEN: Is she very sick?

DIANA: Well, yes, I think so. She underwent a serious operation yesterday—three hours on the operating table. For a while there it was touch and go. But today she seemed much better and I spoke to her. I stood by her bed and she took my hand and she said to me, "You need an enormous strength of will to live through this. Most people need only one reason to do it. I have three: you, your father, and your grandmother." And suddenly I felt furious. I felt *furious* with her. God, she's always been so strong, the strongest person I know, and I've loved her for it. All of a sudden I felt tricked, I felt like saying to her, "Why don't you live for yourself?" I felt like saying, "I can't take this burden on me! What are you doing to me?" And now suddenly I'm here, being asked to talk about work, and I have nothing to say. I haven't a goddamn thing to say! What do I do? After all, what do I do? Half my life is passed in a fantasy of desire that's focused on leaving my husband and finding some marvelous job . . . At least, my mother worked hard all her life. She raised me when my real father walked out on her, she put me through school, she staked me to my first apartment, she never said no to me for anything. And when I got married she felt she'd accomplished everything. That was the end of the rainbow . . .

DOLORES (*timidly*): What's so terrible, really, your mother saying she lived for all of you? God, that used to be considered a moral virtue. I'm sure lots of men feel the same way, that they live for their families. Most men hate their work . . .

MARILYN: My husband used to say that all the time, that he lived only for me and the baby, that that was everything to him.

LUCIE: How did you feel about that? What did you think of him when he said it?

MARILYN (*flushing*): It used to make me feel peculiar. As though something wasn't quite right with him.

LUCIE (*to Diana*): Did you think something wasn't quite right, when your mother said what she said?

DIANA (*thinking back*): No. It wasn't that something wasn't quite right. It seemed "right," if you know what I mean, for her to be saying that, but terribly wrong suddenly.

LUCIE: That's odd, isn't it? When a man says he lives

for his family it sounds positively unnatural to me. When a woman says it, it sounds so "right." So expected.

LAURA: Exactly. What's pathology in a man seems normal in a woman.

CLAIRE: It comes back, in a sense, to a woman always looking for her identity in her family and a man never, or rarely, really doing that.

MARIE: God, this business of identity! Of wanting it from my work and not looking for it in what my husband does.

JEN: Tell me, do men ever look for their identities in their wives' work?

VERONICA: Yes, and then we call them Mr. Streisand. (*Everybody breaks up, and suddenly cookies and fruit are being devoured. Everyone stretches and one or two women walk around the room. After fifteen minutes . . .*)

MARIE (*peeling an orange, sitting yogi-fashion on the floor*): I first went to work for a small publicity firm. They taught me to be a copywriter, and I loved it from the start. I never had any trouble with the people in that firm. It was like one big happy family there. We all worked well with each other and everyone knew a bit about everybody else's work. When the place folded and they let me go I was so depressed, and so *lost*. For the longest time I couldn't even go out looking for a job. I had no sense of how to go about it. I had no real sense of myself as having a transferable skill, somehow. I didn't seem to know how to deal with Madison Avenue. I realized then that I'd somehow never taken that job as a period of preparation for independence in the world. It was like a continuation of my family. As long as I was being taken care of I functioned, but when I was really on my own I folded up. I just didn't know how to operate . . . And I still don't really. It's never been the same. I've never had a job in which I felt I was really operating responsibly since that time.

SHEILA: Do you think maybe you're just waiting around to get married?

MARIE: No, I don't. I know I really want to work, no matter what. I know that I want some sense of myself that's not related to a husband, or to anyone but myself, for that matter . . . But I feel so lost, I just don't know where it's all at, really.

(*Five or six heads nod sympathetically.*)

CLAIRE: I don't feel like *any* of you. Not a single one.

DOLORES: What do you mean?

CLAIRE: Let me tell you something. I have two sisters and a brother. My father was a passionately competitive man. He loved sports and he taught us all how to play, and he treated us all exactly as though we were his equals at it. I mean, he competed with us exactly as though we were twenty-five when we were eight. Everything: sailing, checkers, baseball, there was nothing he wouldn't compete in. When I was a kid I saw him send a line drive ball right into my sister's stomach, for God's sake. Sounds terrible, right? We loved it. All of us. And we thrived on it. For me, work is like everything else. *Competitive.* I can get in there, do the best I can, compete ferociously against man, woman, or machine. And I use whatever I have in the way of equipment: sex, brains, endurance. You name it, I use it. And if I lose I lose, and if I win I win. It's just doing it as well as I can that counts. And if I come up against discrimination as a woman, I just reinforce my attack. But the name of the game is competition.

(*Everyone stares at her, open-mouthed, and suddenly everyone is talking at once; over one another's voices; at one another; to themselves; laughing; interrupting; generally exploding.*)

LAURA (*dryly*): The American dream. Right before our eyes.

DIANA (*tearfully*): Good God, Claire, that sounds awful!

LUCIE (*amazed*): That's the kind of thing that's killing our men. In a sense, it's really why we're here.

SHEILA (*mad*): Oh, that love of competition!

MARIE (*astonished*): The whole idea of just *being* is completely lost in all this.

JEN (*outraged*): And to act *sexy* in order to compete! You degrade every woman alive!

VERONICA (*interested*): In other words, Claire, you imply that if they give you what you want they get *you?*

DIANA (*wistfully*): That notion of competition is everything we hate most in men, isn't it? It's responsible for the most brutalizing version of masculinity. We're in here trying to be men, right? Do we want to be men at their worst?

LUCIE (*angrily*): For God's sake! We're in here trying to be *ourselves*. Whatever that turns out to be.

MARILYN (*with sudden authority*): I think you're wrong, all of you. You don't understand what Claire's really saying. (*Everyone stops talking and looks at Marilyn.*) What Claire is really telling you is that her father taught her not how to win but how to lose. He didn't teach her to ride roughshod over other people. He taught her how to get up and walk away intact when other people rode roughshod over *her*. And he so loved the idea of teaching that to his children that he ignored the fact that she and her sisters were girls, and he taught it to them, anyway. (*Everyone takes a moment to digest this.*)

LAURA: I think Marilyn has a very good point there. That's exactly what Claire has inside her. She's the strongest person in this room, and we've all known it for a long time. She has the most integrated and most *separate* sense of herself of anyone I know. And I can see now that that probably has developed from her competitiveness. It's almost as though it provided the proper relation to other people, rather than no relation.

SHEILA: Well, if that's true then her father performed a minor miracle.

JEN: You're not kidding. Knowing where *you* stand in relation to other people, what you're supposed to be doing, not because of what other people want of you but because of what you want for yourself . . . *knowing* what you want for yourself . . . that's everything, isn't it?

LAURA: *I* think so. When I think of work, that's really what I think of most. And when I think of *me* and work, I swear I feel like Ulysses after ten years at sea. I, unlike the rest of you, do not feel I am where I am because of luck or accident or through the natural striving caused by a healthy competitiveness. I feel I am like a half-maddened bull who keeps turning and turning and turning, trying to get the hell out of this maze he finds himself in . . . I spent ten years not knowing what the hell I wanted to do with myself. So I kept getting married and having children. I've had three children and as many husbands. All nice men, all good to me, all meaningless to me. (*She stops short and seems to be groping for words.*) I wanted to do something. Something that was real, and serious, and would involve me in a struggle with myself. Every time I got married it was like applying Mercurochrome to a festering wound. I swear sometimes I think the thing I resent most is that women have always gotten married as a way out of the struggle. It's the thing we're encouraged to do, it's the thing we rush into with such *relief*, it's the thing we come to absolutely hate. Because marriage itself, for most women, is so full of self-hatred. A continual unconscious reminder of all our weakness, of the heavy price to be paid for taking the easy way out. Men talk about the power of a woman in the home. That power has come to seem such a lopsided and malevolent thing to me. What kind of nonsense is that anyway, to divide up the *influences* on children's lives in that bizarre way? The mother takes care of the *emotional* life of a child? The vital requirement for nourishment? Out of what special resources does she do that? What the hell principle of growth is operating in her? What gives a woman who never tests herself against structured work the wisdom or the self-discipline to oversee a child's emotional development? The whole thing is crazy, just crazy. And it nearly drove me crazy . . . What can I say? For ten years I felt as though I were continually vomiting up my life . . . And now I work. I work hard and I work with great relish. I want to have a family, too. Love. Home.

Husband. Father for the children. Of course, I do. God, the loneliness! The longing for connection! But work first. And family second. (*Her face splits wide open in a big grin.*) Just like a man.

LUCIE: I guess I sort of feel like Laura. Only I'm not sure. I'm not sure of anything. I'm in school now. Or rather "again." Thirty years old and I'm a graduate student again, starting out almost from scratch . . . The thing is I could never take what I was doing seriously. That is, not as seriously as my brother, or any of the boys I went to school with, did. Everything seemed too long, or too hard, or too something. Underneath it all, I felt sort of *embarrassed* to study seriously. It was as if I was really feeling: "That's something the *grownups* do. It's not something for *me* to do." I asked my brother about this feeling once, and he said most men felt the same way about themselves, only they fake it better than women do. I thought about that one a long time, and I kept trying to say to myself: What the hell, it's the same for them as it is for us. But . . . (*she looks swiftly around the circle*) it's not! Dammit, it's *not*. After all, style is content, right? And ours are worlds away . . .

VERONICA: Literally.

LUCIE: I don't know . . . I still don't know. It's a problem that nags and nags and nags at me. So often I wish some guy would just come along and I'd disappear into marriage. It's like this secret wish that I can just withdraw from it all, and then from my safe position look on and comment and laugh and say yes and no and encourage and generally play at being the judging mother, the "wise" lady of the household. But then I know within six months I'd be miserable! I'd be climbing the walls and feeling guilty . . .

MARILYN: Guilty! Guilty, guilty. Will we *ever* have a session in which the word guilty is not mentioned once? (*Outside, the bells in a nearby church tower strike midnight.*)

DIANA: Let's wrap it up, okay?

VERONICA (*reaching for her bag*): Where shall we meet next week?

MARIE: Wait a minute! Aren't we going to sum up? (*Everyone stops in mid-leaving, and sinks wearily back into her seat.*)

LUCIE: Well, one thing became very clear to me. Every one of us in some way has struggled with the idea of getting married in order to be relieved of the battle of finding and staying with good work.

DIANA: And every one of us who's actually done it has made a mess of it!

JEN: And everyone who *hasn't* has made a mess of it!

VERONICA: But, look. The only one of us who's really worked well—with direction and purpose—is Claire. And we all jumped on her! (*Everyone is startled by this observation, and no one speaks for a long moment.*)

MARILYN (*bitterly*): We can't do it, we can't admire anyone who *does* do it, and we can't let it alone . . .

JEN (*softly*): That's not quite true. After all, we were able to see finally that there was virtue in Claire's position. And we are here, aren't we?

MARIE: That's right. Don't be so down. We're not a hundred and two years old, are we? We're caught in a mess, damned if we do and damned if we don't. All right. That's exactly why we're here. To break the bind. (*On this note everyone takes heart, brightens up, and troops out into the darkened Manhattan streets. Proof enough of being ready to do battle.*)

21

On Trial for Acting like a Man

The facts of the case are these: In 1967 Gabrielle Russier, a divorced woman of thirty, the mother of nine-year-old twins, and the possessor of a brilliant academic record from the University of Aix-en-Provence, became a teacher of French literature in a high school in Marseilles. She was, in authoritarian France, unusual in that she considered her students people, saw life from their point of view, and drew close to them both as a friend and as a teacher. They, in turn, adored her, called her "Gatito" (little cat in Spanish), and addressed her with the familiar *tu*. Among her students was a boy of sixteen named Christian Rossi. Christian, a tall, husky, bearded young man, was a passionate Maoist and the son of two professors at the University of Aix-en-Provence (which is almost a suburb of Marseilles). Both Mr. and Mrs. Rossi were Communists, and Mr. Rossi had been Gabrielle Russier's teacher. The boy Christian and the woman

Gabrielle became intimate friends, and in June 1968, after the May uprising, they fell in love and began an affair.

Toward the end of that summer Gabrielle went to Christian's father and told him of her love for his son and of her desire to live openly with Christian. Professor Rossi flew into a rage and became determined to part the lovers. When this began to seem impossible—there were terrible raging scenes between father and son and the son finally ran away from home—the Rossis filed a complaint in court and Gabrielle was arrested for corruption of a minor. (By this time Christian was seventeen and Gabrielle thirty-one.) Gabrielle was imprisoned in Marseilles for a number of months under the law of preventive detention. At last, in July 1969, she came to trial in a closed court and was given a suspended sentence, which amounted to amnesty. Half an hour later, as a result of a telephone call from the Public Ministry, the prosecuting attorney gave Gabrielle's lawyer the astonishing news that the state would appeal the decision in a higher court and seek a stiffer penalty for Gabrielle Russier. The point of this was to make sure she would have a police record, thereby making it impossible for her ever again to teach anywhere in France.

Gabrielle, destroyed by her months in prison and the nightmare that had become her daily existence, broke down entirely and was sent to a convalescent home to await a new trial. She returned to Marseilles—all alone—at the end of the summer, and on September 1, 1969, unable to stop brooding about her ruined life, she committed suicide.

The issues the case of Gabrielle Russier raises are obvious and painful. How could such a thing have happened? Why was she imprisoned? What was her real crime? Could this have happened to her had she been a man? Why were the French authorities determined to ruin her? What is the relation among all these questions?

One reads and rereads the facts of the case, and one falls into the well-developed habit of accepting bizarre premises when presented as an unquestioned starting point. It all becomes so *easy* to understand: then she did this, then he did that, then they were faced with this consequence, then his parents were faced with that consequence, then The Law took over . . . and so it all neatly unfolded, it all followed a weird kind of logic, it all, in retrospect, seems "inevitable." And suddenly one's mind jolts to a stop—she is actually *dead*! it all really *killed* her—and the emotional confusion that then crowds in on the brain wipes out the apparent reasonableness with which one has been "understanding" these events. With bitter lucidity one sees that the death of Gabrielle Russier was the kind of offering demanded by cultural custom in the face of any real challenge to its authority; especially if the challenger is "other."

When I first read of Gabrielle Russier I thought, Clearly this all happened because she was a woman. Then I thought, No, it's more than that, the complication of class figures strongly in this. The outraged French bourgeoisie was determined to punish the renegade in its midst as it would not have punished a man or a woman of either the lower *or* the upper classes. Then I returned to my original conviction: regardless of other factors, Gabrielle Russier would not have been meted out the particular and fatal brand of justice she *did* receive had she not been a woman.

Nevertheless, it was impossible not to wonder why a woman would be put on trial and hounded to death for having slept with a boy in the country that produced a literature of print and film—including *Cheri, The Red and the Black, Devil in the Flesh, The Rules of the Game*—demonstrating repeatedly that women of forty have slept with boys of eighteen from time immemorial in order to initiate them properly into the life of the senses. Also, one wondered, how could this happen in a country that respects the achievement of its exceptional women as inordinately as France does? In France, a woman who possesses a first-rate intelligence is taken seriously much more commonly than in other Western countries, and once her ability becomes apparent she often rises to high position without the opposition she eternally faces elsewhere.

Why, then, Gabrielle Russier?

The answer, in the first instance, lies in two words: *outraged secrecy.* The very point of all these "inappropriate" liaisons—when they occur between a boy and a woman—is that they take place in dead secrecy; the power of the older woman lies in her skillful manipulation of some easily labeled position—distant relative, friend of the family, trustworthy neighbor—secretly, never, under any circumstances, losing the essential operating tool of respectability. It is a game of odds: if the woman plays the odds well she is released into mastery; if she plays badly she forfeits everything up to and sometimes including her life. Nowhere in French literature are we taught these lessons so well as in *Les Liaisons Dangereuses*. Gabrielle Russier chose not to play any odds. She chose to live openly with her offensively young lover. In short: she lost her head.

As for the second instance, women of high accomplishment are rewarded because the overriding passion of the French *in cultural power* is intellectual attainment. Any eccentricity or freakishness or flouting of the rules will be tolerated in France if it should emerge in an intellectual who compels admiration. I sometimes think an ape could become president of France if it had a Ph.D. in Sanskrit. Unfortunately, Gabriel Russier was a high school teacher of sufficient but not remarkable intelligence. She never qualified.

The truth, then, of the position of women in France is that those who glitter brilliantly and manipulate the system successfully are a direct reflection of the shocking powerlessness of all those who do not. It was the prosecuting attorney who said that "if she had been a hairdresser, or if she had slept with a young apprentice, it would have been different." She would not have been dealt with so harshly. She would not have been dealt with at all. But Gabrielle was not a hairdresser. To a significant degree she was considered a keeper of the culture: an educated woman of the most unbending middle class in the Western world, a middle class of vicious self-importance, a middle class that operates with extraordinary skill and talent inside a rigid set of behavioral rules and plays the Queen of Hearts without mercy when those rules are challenged, especially if they are challenged by a woman. When there was an uproar over the state's appeal for a stiffer sentence for Gabrielle, the Public Ministry said it was only routine, while a hundred Parisian lawyers said, "Never! This kind of appeal hasn't been made ten times in the last forty years, and never has it been made for a charge such as this one."

Gabrielle Russier went on trial then, in the court of public opinion, for acting like a man—and for this brazenness was punished inordinately. One of the vital concerns that arose out of the Russier trial was the question of the law of preventive detention, under which someone charged with a crime can remain in prison for incredible periods of time awaiting trial. Well, thousands of "hairdressers" languish in preventive detention all the time. Who on earth would or could take action on their behalf? But that a woman of Gabrielle's class should so languish. Unheard of. Yet she did.

Gabrielle was being charged both by public opinion and the government with every obscenity imaginable. Not for having committed an actual crime, not with a set of legally damaging facts, not with vice, fraud, arson, or murder, but rather with being a fallen woman. She was charged with having slept with a man fifteen years younger than herself. She was charged with being a whore, a nymphomaniac, a threat to public morality, a bad mother, a divorced woman. (In Mavis Gallant's memorable phrase, *"Divorced woman* clanged away with the regularity of a clock striking.") She was charged, in the final analysis, with having an insufficient character in the view of Parisian shopkeepers as well as in the view of the Public Ministry. (A lawyer in Paris said, "It is not the machinery of the law that is crushing her. It is only a few men with opinions.") She was charged, in effect, with not having a proper "soul." It was for all of this that she died.

In *The Stranger*, Albert Camus's character, Meursault, is also tried for not having the proper soul. He is not being judged guilty for the actual crime of having murdered someone, but for his inability to feel remorse, for his sacrilegious attitude toward his mother, for his insupportable separateness in the human community.

Years ago, a movie called *La Vérité* demonstrated the same French penchant for judgment according to some bourgeois assessment of character rather than according to criminal code. In the movie, a woman goes on trial not really for the actuality of her crime but for the immorality of her past, the number of lovers she has had, the general distastefulness of her character. In her essay about the trial of Gabrielle Russier, Mavis Gallant points out that it is not likely in an actual court of French law that Meursault would have been tried for the contents of his soul; on the other hand, it *is* likely that the woman in the movie would have been so tried. She recounts a series of cases in French law where women on trial hear judges say things like "I have searched everywhere in the record for your soul, and I am unable to find it"; where a man charged with murder received eight years and the woman who supposedly incited him to commit the crime received twelve years, where a woman charged with murder was sentenced not because the facts against her were incontrovertible but because the judge was horrified by the number of lovers she had had (saying her life would tempt the pen of a Balzac) and he disapproved of the books she had read. Gallant, a Canadian writer who has lived in France for many years, states categorically that it would be unheard of in the trial of a man that judgment of this sort be brought to bear in lieu of the bare facts. What men cannot bear to inflict on themselves they will often easily inflict on a woman.

After Gabrielle's death a New York publisher put together a book telling the story of the schoolboy and the teacher; it is composed of an introductory essay by Mavis Gallant; a shorter preface by Raymond Jean, a teacher and friend of Gabrielle's; and the letters from prison written by Gabrielle herself. Gallant's essay is brilliant; not another word need be said on the trial and its meaning for French society after one has read it. She tells the story of the two lovers from every necessary point of view: hers, his, the parents, the magistrates, the law, national customs, the power of French patriarchy, the influence of literature, the academic life in which the principals moved, the influence of the May '68 uprisings—it is all satisfyingly, abundantly, sadly, ironically viewed through the eyes of a remarkably informed foreigner.

Raymond Jean is less interesting. A French Communist and a former professor of Gabrielle's at the University of Aix-en-Provence, his personal memoir serves to sketch in the character of the protagonists in this deathly melodrama, but he grows tiresome, railing endlessly against the "bourgeois courts." It is the letters of Gabrielle herself that are the most penetrating part of the book. At first calm, lively, literate, they fall gradually into a depthless despair; it is the despair of a woman who in her wildest nightmares never dreamed that her life could descend into such stunning negation.

What nags at the heart, though, long after one has stopped reading these letters, is the vivid evocation of Gabrielle among the other prisoners, sinking deeper and deeper each day into the kind of bottomless humiliation from which one rarely recovers, and was surely at the center of the suicidal depression that caused her to take her own life. After all, as the noble Anton Chekhov said, "It is important that a human being never be humiliated. That is the main thing."

22

The Women's Movement in Crisis

On Tuesday, November 4, the people of New York State will go to the polls to vote on whether or not the Equal Rights Amendment should be added to the constitution. The amendment requests that "Equality of rights under the law shall not be denied or abridged by the State of New York or any subdivision thereof on account of sex." The vote is important because if New York votes yes to the ERA, not only will it make the women of the state equal under the law, it will provide other states with the impetus to vote yes also, thereby moving us ever closer to achieving the ratification by three-fourths of the states necessary for a Constitutional amendment to pass. If and when this happens, the women of this country, after more than a century of struggle, will be declared legal persons equal with men before the law of the land.

The vote is also important for even more fundamental reasons. Its campaign—both for and against—has brought to the surface a significant amount of gratifying support as well as a reprisal of the age-old quarrel conservative Americans have always had with women's rights. The amount of anti-ERA campaigning: alarming in 1975. To think, after nearly ten years of steadily growing feminist thought and action the opposition in this country is still so simple-minded and so ignorant that it can instruct its followers that ERA means women will have to go to the bathroom with men, women will be forced to work, women will be forced to contribute 50 percent of all household expenses, and so on, *ad nauseam*. On the other hand, there has been a tremendous amount of positive response from people who did little or nothing about the ERA in previous years. Organizations of all sorts, politicians at every level, ordinary citizens, have joined in a genuine coalition to help the ERA pass in New York. It is exciting and heart lifting to observe this true citizens' effort in service to women's rights.

But this vote is, in my view, most important because it has given rise to a peculiar debate within the women's movement itself. That debate can be summarized as follows: "The women's movement seems to be falling apart. The organizations are dying, our ranks are split and fragmented, we are involved in the most dreadful internecine warfare, absolutely nothing seems to be happening, the only thing we are all able to rally around is the ERA. Only five years ago we were involved in large and profound issues, and now all we seem to have left is this old warhorse. It is exactly like the visionary feminists of the nineteenth century being gradually reduced to the issue of suffrage . . . Is *this* what we have been fighting for? Is this *all* that it has all been about?"

I would like here to enter *my* argument in the debate.

To begin with, it should be useful rather than disheartening to compare ourselves with the nineteenth-century feminists; if we look long and hard at this comparison, we will see that the differences between us are more compelling than the samenesses, and those differences, of necessity, lead this generation of feminists to different conclusions. In the nineteenth century the feminists stood alone; they had no one but themselves and each other; the world was massively aligned against them; they could not make a dent in the ordinary culture.

This isolation produced two important results: on the one hand, it insured the unbroken solidarity that nurtures revolutionary thought; on the other hand, it insured the cumulative weariness that comes from banging your head against a stone wall for forty years, the one that disintegrates the most dedicated of true believer efforts. Thus, women like Lucretia Mott and Susan B. Anthony became truly great theoreticians and leaders—and in the end had nothing to lead but the fight for the vote.

We, on the other hand, born into a significantly different world, have everything to lead—but we have no leaders. We have not produced—and I prophesy will not produce—the intellectually coherent leadership that characterized nineteenth-century feminism. But paradoxically, we have, in less than a decade, made our voices heard throughout the land, persuaded thousands of people of the rightness of our cause, forced government to respond to our demands, and put into the world a piece of consciousness that will not—cannot—be gone back on.

In short: they of the nineteenth century were the children of the socially conscious segment of the Victorian upper classes. We are the children of the grass-roots, egalitarian twentieth century. We are profoundly different people living in profoundly different times. It is impossible that what we make and do and live through should ever simply amount to a repeat of their history. Each set of feminists has its own merits and limitations, and each set makes a vital and distinctive contribution to the struggle as a whole.

We are a genuinely broad-based movement that is dependent for its life not on the existence of a structured leadership but on the internalized awareness that each and every one of us in her own person, her own work, her own life—is a force for feminist dissemination. We talk about reaching the people. We forget: we *are* the people. Every feminist, wittingly or unwittingly, is an organizer at large among the people. Every feminist every moment of her principled life is increasing, osmotically, the social atmosphere in which the gathering force for change takes root.

And it is happening, it is happening. All over this country, in small towns and cities, in places where they never heard of Betty Friedan, where they know nothing of Gloria Steinem or the Redstockings, the women are changing, the tiny daily challenges increase, the bravery of independent thought flourishes. I have traveled this country many times in the last five years. I have listened to housewives, students, factory workers, and postal clerks—women who would hesitate to call themselves feminists who, nevertheless, speak about themselves and their lives in ways that would have been unthinkable ten years ago; ways that clearly indicate a growing sense of self that of necessity is producing a radically different generation of women-in-the-world.

A year ago a housewife in Iowa wrote to her cousin in New York:

Although I think I am a typical suburban housewife, I don't think any of my friends would call me typical. I like to read, teach part-time, worked hard for McGovern, adopted a black child, and, yes, at dinner parties I challenge some of the "male chauvinist" attitudes. (Man: "Women doing the dishes is just a natural division of labor." Me: "Not natural, *learned*.") This sort of thing makes me somewhat different. I'm not quite a misfit, but I don't quite fit in.

Our neighborhood has a homeowners' association that faces periodic crisis. One night I was arguing for a particular course of action, I looked around and realized I'm the only woman who ever says anything at the meetings. It honestly never dawned on me before, but I suddenly saw the truth: nobody expects the women to talk. It bothers them all—especially the men—when a woman talks.

I met a new friend whose husband is a radiologist (smart, right?). Word reached me through the grapevine that this man was uncomfortable around me because I was too smart. I had *never even held* a conversation with him.

This woman, at the end of her letter, said—sweetly, superfluously—that she has not joined any organized groups but that she is definitely in sympathy with the women's movement.

Now, certainly, it is true that if it had not been for the development of an organized women's movement this woman would never have written this letter. But it is also true that the organized women's movement is no longer guiding her political destiny. There is in this letter clear evidence of a developing self that already has a life of its own. We, the organized movement, helped bring this power of independent thought into the world, but it is now often beyond us, out there in political time and space. Nonetheless, the shared consciousness of this new thing in the world is the strength and meaning of feminism today; it is what puts feminism on the map of social revolution, and makes it a thrilling part of the great egalitarian thrust of this century. It is this consciousness, also, that again marks the differences between us and the nineteenth-century feminists. For they stood isolated, their consciousness running upstream against the social currents of their century, and thus everything they said and did and thought stood out in stark relief. We, on the other hand, stand smack in the middle of the deepest social currents of *our* century. Our consciousness is the open floodgate behind which stand ready to run the deepest desires of the time and will now, I believe, run almost regardless of what we in New York and Berkeley and Chicago say and do and think.

For these reasons, the internecine warfare among feminists strikes me as both sad and foolish. At one and the same time, the self-importance to which it speaks seems outrageously off the mark and the lack of generosity behind it indicates a serious waste of useful energy. What happens inside the movement now is important only because those happenings determine whether or not the movement will continue to be an effective instrument for the dissemination of what we have already set in motion; on the other hand, that surge clearly has a life of its own now, one that pays relatively little attention to the quarrels of the New York "leadership," and will proceed on its course with or without us.

It is dismaying, almost tragic, that after a few years of near silence the invaluable group of radical feminists known as the Redstockings—the group that coined the terms "consciousness raising" and "the politics of housework"— should have re-emerged with its great revolutionary energy focused on denouncing Gloria Steinem and *Ms.* magazine as dangerous enemies of the women's movement. Dismaying because bringing charges against Steinem is so wrongheaded an action. (I looked at those tabloid-sized charges and I thought, So young, and already we have our first purge.) Tragic because it is so meaningless an exercise in terms of feminist activity.

This preoccupation with the "betrayal" by *Ms.* magazine that involves so many feminists is typical of the curious kind of helplessness that the movement is inflicting upon itself with its internal quarrels. For after all, what is the reality, finally, of the "traitorousness" of *Ms.*?

A number of years ago, about fifty women gathered in Gloria Steinem's living room to discuss the possibility of starting a feminist magazine. The women in that room occupied every space on the feminist political spectrum I'd ever heard of and some I'd never heard of. Everyone had different ideas and different approaches to the question of a feminist magazine. I, for instance, wanted to start a newspaper that would resemble Susan B. Anthony's *Revolution* and would be given over to good, strong writing. Others wanted to start a glossy magazine that would appeal to all those women "out there." I wanted to finance my newspaper through feminist contributions; others wanted to "rip off the Establishment for $9 million." The exchange went on for hours. Meanwhile, at one end of the room sat a number of well-dressed women quietly jotting figures on paper: women who *clearly* knew how capitalist enterprise works. The upshot was I (and everyone else like me) walked away from that meeting, went back to my working life, and forgot about the magazine.

Gloria Steinem and her friends with the pieces of paper went seriously at it, and the result was *Ms.*

It was inevitable that *Ms.* would reflect the style, personality, taste, and politics of those who ran it. It could not reflect the style, personality, taste, and politics of those who walked out of that room. Steinem and *Ms.* could do nothing but become themselves. That self, as it turned out, was not my self, or the self of many other feminists. The magazine proved to be slick, conservative, philistine (Ellen Willis hit the nail on the head when she said *Ms.* was interested in editors, not in writers). Its intellectual level is very low, its sense of the women "out there" patronizing, its feminist politics arrested at the undergraduate level.

For many of us the magazine was a great disappointment. For others, disappointment escalated into anger. For still others, anger developed into flaming belligerence and the conviction that the magazine was distorting and betraying the movement.

For myself, I could never figure out what all this fuss was about. After all, I thought, what the hell did *Ms.* owe me? Nothing. If I didn't like the magazine I was free to organize another one. And as far as the movement was concerned, did *Ms.* "own" the movement that it could distort and betray it? The movement had embraced as many different political positions as there were feminists; this kind of tolerance was a vital strength; why should it now be that if the politics of this magazine was dangerous to me? If *Ms.* existed did that mean I did not exist? If *Ms.* had a following did that mean that my friends and I did not have a following? If *Ms.*'s feminism was not my feminism did that mean it was "the enemy"? Surely, that way lay the oldest political madness in the world.

The women who run *Ms.* are not my political sisters or my working colleagues or my bosom pals. I cannot make natural community with them. Their view of the world is not my view of the world, their values are not my values. For all that, they are feminists—and as such we are allies in the larger cause that binds us all together.

Gloria Steinem and *Ms.* are not the enemy. The enemy is sexism. The enemy is the absence of feminist consciousness. The enemy is all those who actively hate and deny the growing autonomy of women.

That we should be calling each other the enemy instead of keeping our eyes on the real target is a cause for sorrow and alarm. The Old Left at least partially destroyed itself because the socialists and the communists were involved for so long and so bitter a time in savaging each other. If we in the feminist movement repeat this fatal pattern of political behavior we will turn ourselves over lock, stock, and consciousness to our deepest insecurities—and hence to that weakening from within that the real enemy only profits from.

And in the name of what is all this happening? And toward what end? We are only midwives; the baby is already born; it is true, it is only a weak, squalling infant, and possibly, without nourishment or care of any kind, it may die. But babies are sturdy creatures; once given a taste of life they cling to it, fight for it, pretty much make their way in the world.

The fight for the ERA is important—but not that important. It can never—not in the next thousand years—mean what fighting for the vote at the end of the nineteenth century meant. That fight was the signal that the war was over, and the feminists had lost; the vote was the territorial bone thrown the vanquished by the victor. The ERA means exactly the opposite: the war is on its way to being won, and the recalcitrance over the ERA is a last-ditch stand made by a steadily losing side. If the ERA does not pass this year, it will pass next year. Of that there can no longer be any doubt.

Which does not mean that we sit back and not campaign, or worse yet, not go to the polls. We must call every shot every damned day of our lives; we must struggle over every law, protest over every daily discrimination, march endlessly to Albany and Washington, challenge every man at every dinner table, fight for jobs, credit, housing, and the equal care of children.

But: understand all the while what it is we are fighting for, what the nature of that struggle is, and what the real position of each and every one of us is in that struggle.

The campaign this year for the ERA gives us a chance to see that while we've come far, we still have a very long way to go. So we plunge back in and keep on slogging. The real question for me is: On that long trudge ahead who will give me more sustenance, the housewife from Iowa or my leaders in the movement? At the moment I'd say the housewife. The housewife, living in her small community "out there," daily risks becoming a pariah for the sake of her growing feminism. For my money, *she* is the brave soldier in the army of the revolution. My leaders in New York are in danger of being conned by their own press releases into forgetting that revolution, like art, is neither agony nor ecstasy but mainly sheer hard work; work done always in the service of The Cause which, when it is really gathering steam, does not separate the leaders out from the followers.

No one of us has "the truth," or the word, or the correct view, or the only way. Each feminist is a microcosm of feminism, and as discrete as each one's feminism is, it *still* contains the whole of things. That is the glory of the movement at its best; that is what makes us so intensely a part of our time; that is the life within I think we should fight very hard to protect.

23

Why Do these Men Hate Women?

Last month Grove Press published a book called *Genius and Lust: A Journey Through the Major Writings of Henry Miller*, by Norman Mailer. The book was reviewed widely, with varying amounts of attention given to a fresh appraisal of Henry Miller. Richard Gilman's review in the *Village Voice* paid more attention to the relationship between Miller's writings and Norman Mailer's running commentary, recognizing accurately that the relationship between the two was what, in fact, the book was all about. The underlying tone of Gilman's review was: "As an *au courant* person, I know this book will drive the feminists up the wall but, gee, fellas, it's really pretty terrific stuff, anyway." That tone, together with the publication of the book, speaks to an attitude that, in 1976, remains essentially unchanged, insisting that certain truths about life and art are timeless; that, misogyny notwithstanding, the work of both these men remains hungry and alive, telling us something urgent about what it is to be human.

I find that insistence remarkable. I find it remarkable because it simply is not true. Certainly, in the case of Norman Mailer it is not true; nor is it true in the case of those American writers who most resemble Mailer in that misogyny is at the heart of their work. Not true at all. On the contrary: what *is* true is that misogyny is the characteristic mark of the arrested nature of their work, the regressiveness at the center of their books.

As for Henry Miller, what can one say? Miller has often been (and is again in these reviews) compared with Louis-Ferdinand Céline, the great French nihilist writing at the same time as Miller—obsessing about Jews while Miller obsessed about women—and producing the same kind of mad, blazing, hate-filled beauty on the page. I used to think: I must be more of a woman than a Jew because I can read Céline but I can't read Miller. But the fact is that Céline is by far the greater of the two writers. In a curious way his larger talent turns on the all inclusiveness of his nihilism. Céline's self-hatred is as great as his hatred of others; his own anguish is felt, his own mad pain descends into a swamp of loathing that hits and mingles with the general currents of self-hatred that were about to engulf Europe in the thirties, and it transforms his work into radiant poison.

With Miller it is an altogether other matter. In Miller, one feels a tone of separating self-regard at work: "You geeks, you cunts, you freaks and whores, I may look like all the rest of you but I'm not! I'm different, better, more sensitive. My lust is of higher order. Its sheer giganticism sets me apart."

This difference between Céline and Miller is perhaps the difference between Europe and America; Céline knows better; *everyone* is down there in the pits. Miller really thinks he takes Bunyanesque steps across the world of human vermin. This belief is at the heart of his work; it is responsible for both his power and his severe limitations. It is also the essence of the adolescent psyche that has dominated the work of many American writers, Miller being only one of the most prominent. And there is, undeniably, something powerful and admirable in this spitting, hissing, yowling insistence, this American self-regard that will be goddamned fucked if it will simply take its properly world-weary place in the universe. Miller stands up there in Rabelaisian sprawl and yells into the black surround: "Goddamn you, world, I *exist*." When it works, this is infantilism transformed, invested with mythic properties. But it often doesn't work and, when it doesn't, it is merely infantilism.

The natural state of the infantile psyche is one of self-absorption. In this state, other people are only projected images of the self's own need, its own fantasies, its own blood-congested urgencies. Above all, other people are projected images of its own fears: dreadful fears of mortality. These fears must, at all costs, be conquered, otherwise life is unlivable. It is a function of emotional infantilism that it imagines the way to conquer fear is to conquer the people who embody it.

In Henry Miller, those who must be conquered are, of course, women. And the lengths to which Miller goes to conquer these projected images of fear, hunger, and need know no bounds. The degradation in which he steeps himself and the unreality of his women are just short of insane.

Yet Miller's work carries with it the insistent power of this central life fever truly felt, truly expressed. This is because Miller's work is profoundly of its time: a time when this lusting, enraged, adolescent ego hit a receptive nerve in American life and history. The time and the work found deep reverberations in each other. Each knew exactly as much about itself as the other did: no more, no less.

What Miller and the thirties knew about themselves and each other is no longer what writers and the seventies know. Therefore, those writers who continue to echo the misogyny of Henry Miller as though it contained a metaphysical knowledge of the self are arrested in their development, wildly off the map of cultural time, living inside a sensibility that is no longer instinct with the subterranean truths of world and being as most of us are experiencing them. These writers are isolated from our life, and they do not know it.

Norman Mailer is, of course, the most glaring example of such a writer. I have grown up with Norman Mailer's misogyny, and it did not always seem so dismaying to me as it does now. But it *was* not always so dismaying. Take a story like "The Time of Her Time"—as woman-hating a tale as anyone could wish for. Yet, most of us read it with as much amazement and complicitous laughter as outrage. This because Mailer's own sweating, lunging, disheveled, despairing sexual fantasies were so nakedly at work that he drew you into his anguish, made his dilemma one of general human appeal: you shared the condition; you were all helpless, ridiculous human beings together.

Two things have happened since "The Time of Her Time." One, my ability to "identify" with the Mailer protagonist has altered forever; I can no longer make common cause with the men in Mailer's woman-objectifying melodramas. Two, Mailer has remained fixed in his literary mode of sexual antagonism which, even as the life within it evaporates decade by decade, he coldly, somewhat hysterically insists on raising to the level of religious ceremony.

Mailer has never understood that stories like "The Time of Her Time" can *only* be a function of emotional adolescence. He figured it worked for a lifetime for Miller and Hemingway, why not for him? He has not seen, and to this day does not see, that it worked for those two supreme American swaggerers only as long as the culture as a whole also subscribed to the same adolescent truths about men and women and experienced these truths as a metaphor for life itself. When the culture no longer did, and Miller and Hemingway themselves could not grow and mature, their writing lives were over, and they both declined into self-parody.

For Mailer, unlike Miller and Hemingway, it was to some extent over almost before it began. He did not grasp the importance of the thirty years' lapse between his time and theirs, and he descended into self-parody much earlier than either of the other two. That is why he never wrote the "great" book expected of him and, in all probability, never will. By the time he was writing *An American Dream*, he was lost to a psychological sense of things which, more often than not, was turned in upon itself, not reflecting the truth of our lives at all, speaking to private wishes, private fears. This deluded sense of things has always, without exception, turned on the elaborate structure of his misogyny. It is in his misogyny that Mailer is most regressive, most at a distance from the creation of live literature.

Mailer's misogyny is trapped inside a mythic terminology that is presented as though it were cosmic truth. The essence of this mythology may be found in the following sentence from *The Prisoner of Sex:*

> So do men look to destroy every quality in a woman which will give her the powers of a male, for she is in their eyes already armed with the power that she brought them forth, and that is a power beyond measure—the earliest etchings of memory go back to that woman between whose legs they were conceived, nurtured, and near-strangled in the hours of birth.

That, says Mailer in all of his books, is at the heart of what passes between human beings who are men and women.

> The human being who is a man can encounter the human being who is a woman in one way only: he must mount her, fuck her, suck her, penetrate and impale her, conquer and reduce her, for she is not simply another human being like himself but rather the embodiment of the mysterious heart—the universal elemental source—

and it is only through that raging lust, in that Cosmic Fuck that he can hope to close with the Mysteries of the Inner Space thus reducing her powers and increasing his own.

That, says Mailer, is the truth about men and women, and all the rest is totalitarian bullshit. And don't you ever forget it, you Shock Troops of the Liberation, you pathetic dumb-cunt broads (uh excuse me, you Great Female Power of the Universe).

It is now abundantly clear that Mailer will probably go on speaking this sorrowful male-female nonsense, with no more wisdom than he had twenty-five years ago, until he is in his doddering seventies. A number of the passages in Mailer's commentary in *Genius and Lust* were taken word for word from *The Prisoner of Sex*, an essay Mailer wrote in 1971. Mailer reproduces those sentences five years later without the slightest trace of irony or self-consciousness, as though the sentiments behind them are exactly as true for him today as they were then. Here are some samples:

Miller captured something in the sexuality of men as it had never been seen before, precisely that it was man's sense of awe before woman, his dread of her position one step closer to eternity (for in that step were her powers) which made men detest women, revile them, humiliate them, defecate symbolically upon them, do everything to reduce them so that one might dare to enter them and take pleasure of them.

And, conversely, Miller

> screams his barbaric yawp of utter adoration for the
> power and the glory and the grandeur of the female in
> the universe, and it is his genius to show that this power
> is ready to survive any context or abuse.

What is one to do with such writing? Who does Mailer
imagine such language speaks to? Is it possible he thinks
women will recognize any element of themselves—real or
imagined—in these ludicrous and dehumanizing descriptions? And, I wonder, how many men are there left who
recognize *themselves* in these descriptions? Is the sexual
obsession that passes here for myth really central to our lives?

I, for one, say no. It seems to me that the writers with the
least to say today are obsessed with a myth of male-female
sexuality that daily presents itself as an ever more foolish,
ever more falsifying construct. Worse: this myth now
sounds downright fascist. Racists, from the Ku Klux Klan
to Hitler, used the same kind of mythifying rhetoric in
order that they might oppress and destroy blacks and Jews:
If women are not simply other human beings, if they are
indeed possessed of frightening powers, then one stands in
awe of them in order that one might strike them down. It is
a classic mechanism of oppression, one that is *always* offered
as an insight into cosmic truth.

Not only is the truth of our lives not to be found in this
construct, but, more and more, there is less and less art to
be found in it. Mailer himself says in his Miller commentary that what "separates the artist from everyone else who

works at being one . . . is that the artist has risen precisely from therapy to art . . . the artist's ultimate interest is to put something together which is independent of the ego." Indeed. Mailer knows whereof he speaks. The struggle between therapy and art is spread generously across the pages of his work; it is a struggle he loses more often than he wins.

Within this context, *The Prisoner of Sex* is an important piece of work, a sad piece of work. The essay is divided into two parts: one, an enraged denunciation of the women's movement into which is woven Mailer's cosmic truth about men and women; two, a critical defense of the work of Henry Miller and D. H. Lawrence against what Mailer takes to be Kate Millett's distorting polemic in *Sexual Politics*.

The defense of Miller and Lawrence is eloquent: persuasively reasoned, beautifully written, the work of a fine truth-speaking mind. Especially in the case of Lawrence. Mailer makes live again Lawrence's great power: that devotion in him—to the idea of salvation through the sexual tenderness between men and women—that amounted to emotional genius. Never mind, says Mailer, Lawrence's purple prose, the fascism of his "blood-consciousness," the mean fears of his theories of woman's submission and man's domination—look only to the beauty of his sense of men and women caught together in the richness and terror of being. If you lose that, if you strip that down, if you distort that for the sake of your politics, you lose the meaning of literature, you impoverish life immeasurably. In the writing of these passages Mailer speaks nobly.

In the denunciatory part of the essay he is speaking in his own voice, out of his own art, that art he thinks puts him squarely in the tradition of these writers he is defending. The failure is dismaying. Making full use of that ravening, glutted language that has become his hallmark, abusing and hating women at top speed, the work disintegrates entirely. There is no substance here; there is no wisdom; only a mechanical, driven rhetoric: the rhetoric of therapy rather than the language of art.

There are at least two other widely known writers in this country whose work is as stultified as Mailer's and whose chief symptom of stultification is woman hating: Philip Roth and Saul Bellow. Each of these writers is a man of great talent and intelligence; each of them also increasingly displays the kind of self-absorption that results in emotional stupidity. In the matter of creating art the presence of the last renders the first two as nothing.

Philip Roth began his writing career sixteen years ago with the publication of a collection of stories called *Goodbye, Columbus.* The stories were brilliant and deeply moving. They were filled with character, wisdom, and a luminous sense of the quest for a moral, feeling life. They were everything Tolstoy said a book should be. They made you "weep and laugh and love life more because of it."

Roth never again achieved the control over his work that those stories reflected. What has characterized his work since that time is panic. Sometimes this panic is wildly funny, sometimes viciously bitter, but always it prevents vision: control, transcendence. It is the panic of immature vanity: a writer's preoccupation with the question of self-worth becoming greater than his preoccupation with the world as it enters into him. This confusion, in art, is fatal and, indeed, Roth's books have suffered mightily for it. More and more, it has become apparent that Roth is writing, helplessly, about himself. Not drawing upon the materials of his life to create a fictional world: just talking about himself. And what is the chief element of this obsessive, eaten-up-alive exercise in self-absorption? The hatred of women, nakedly, more desperately in possession of the writers. With each book one sees the horror of a writer who has failed to mature personally, has contrived unsuccessfully to make of that failure a modern myth, and recedes yearly into literary self-delusion. *Portnoy's Complaint* was startling, but *My Life as a Man* was frightening. *Portnoy's Complaint* in Roth's career was the equivalent of "The Time of Her Time" in Mailer's. It was a work so full of wonderful human dishevelment, a work so clearly *about* panic rather than driven by it, that we could not but laugh and anguish together with the dubious Portnoy. The hateful caricatures of women in it were clearly a function of the neurosis of the character and, as such, engaged us, drew us in, demanded and gained our reluctant attention.

With *Portnoy* Roth approached the edge of genuine insight. With *My Life as a Man* he withdrew from that edge, back into emotional darkness. Here there is no distance between character and author. Here the hatred of women is not a function of character illumination but a statement of the author's swamped being. In *Portnoy* the mother and the Monkey are monstrous because Alex Portnoy experiences them as monstrous; in *My Life as a*

Man the wife is monstrous because Roth is saying women are monstrous. When the wife is being beaten to death and she surrenders to the ecstasy of what is happening to her, losing control of language as though of her bladder, screaming, "Die me, die me!" Roth is clearly saying this repellent creature and all those who resemble her—*deserves* to die.

And it is here—from this crucial lack of sympathy, this dehumanizing vileness—that the failure of this book flows. The unacknowledged misogyny of *My Life as a Man* leaks like a slow, inky poison all over its pages, obscuring artistic coherence, disintegrating moral intelligence, making of its true subject something so private and ugly as to be of virtually no use to those men and women who read books in order to love life more.

In his sixtieth year and on the eve of winning the Nobel Prize Saul Bellow wrote the most regressive novel of his distinguished career: *Humboldt's Gift.* Again, regression turned on misogyny. Again, regression could be traced back to an earlier novel in which misogyny was a function of character that had now, in the later novel, become a symptom of the author's self-absorption. The protagonist of *Humboldt* is the protagonist of *Herzog* ten years later. In the earlier novel, the distance between the author and his character created an energizing force that made you run madly with Moses Herzog, searching frantically or his life in the streets of New York, in the beds of women, in the writing of letters to the living and the dead. The women were dreadful caricatures but, still: they served felt life.

Humboldt's Gift, a sprawling, feverish work filled with the jet stream of Bellow's language brilliance, is purportedly about the inability to live a life of significance in contemporary America. For me, this was a supremely unrealized novel and, again, a work soaked through with the self-absorption of the writer, not at all something put together independent of the ego. The protagonist, Charlie Citrine, is a thinly disguised Saul Bellow around whom is gathered an enormous cast of characters. None of them has independent life, each one is a projection of the fears, needs, and disappointments of a self-preoccupied writer claiming, unsuccessfully, that what is true for him is true.

Nowhere in this novel does the bilious quality of projected life—as opposed to felt life—come through more clearly than in the creation of the women. To begin with, the women are uniformly referred to as cunts, broads, chicks, and bimbos. Then, they are all either beautiful or "gorgeous." Then, they are all either thin, cold, intelligent, and castrating (these are always the wife) or they are dark, sensual, and mindless (these are the mistress). These characters are like papier-mâché grotesqueries; figures with little magnets affixed to the backs of them triggering fantasies of hunger and deprivation. The wife figure flashes: Touch me. I will evoke for you everything in life that is perpetually doing you in. The mistress figure flashes: Touch *me*. I will evoke for you everything in life that is perpetually holding out on you.

What we have in the work of these writers is not a vital relation to the forces of our moment but rather an infantile preoccupation with themselves. We have here what is fatal in writers: men who hate and fear the moment in which they are living, men who are in flight from their times, at a profound remove from the inner experience of their time and place, filled with a conservative longing for an inner truth that is no longer *the* truth.

The writer's sensibility is the heightened sensibility, and in it, indeed, lies the world discovered. But the difference between self-inspection and self-absorption is the difference between art and therapy. For me, much of the current work of Mailer, Roth, and Bellow is merely therapy, and at that, the worst, the most childish kind of therapy: not the kind that gets to the bottom of things but rather the kind that hardens its defenses, ritualizes human sacrifice, makes do with a primitive kind of bargaining about who's human and who's not. In the misogyny of these writers lies the deluded ancient dream of frightened men: if she is made less human, I will be made more human.

No great writer succumbs to these fears. No great writer sacrifices the humanity of half the world in order that the half identified with his protagonist may gain more life. One thinks of the women of Hardy, Stendhal, Lawrence, and one wants to weep with shame over the shabbiness and emotional cowardice of the best of American male writers. The Europeans struggled brilliantly to face down the fears of their age, the Americans have not. The Europeans identified need, the Americans wallow in it. Out of the struggle of the Europeans came wisdom and a true record of the life they were living through. Out of the fears of the Americans come lots of smarts but not much wisdom and, increasingly, a failure of the work to mature, to say something valuable to us about our world.

In short: When I read Hardy, Lawrence, or Stendhal, their words compel me because they are filled with live men *and* women, rich with dimension and autonomous being. When I read Mailer, Roth, and the later Bellow, not much lives except the self-absorption of an arrested psyche, the sullen vanities of disappointed men, the forfeited talents of writers who, incapable of struggling through into emotional maturity, have lost the ability to create a compelling fictive universe.

The inability of the writer to mature personally is more crucial in the second half of the twentieth century than it has been at any other time in modern history. Awareness of the self is more acutely at the heart of things than it has ever been before. On the foundation of self-awareness alone rest all our hopes for a new politics, a new society, a revitalized life. If we do not genuinely know ourselves, the void will now, at last, surely rise up to meet us.

24

Toward a Definition
of the Female Sensibility

It is useless to go to the great men writers for help, however much one may go to them for pleasure. Lamb, Browne, Thackeray, Newman, Sterne, Dickens . . . never helped a woman yet, though she may have learnt a few tricks of them and adapted them to her use. The weight, the pace, the stride of a man's mind are too unlike her own for her to lift anything substantial from him success-fully. The ape is too distant to be sedulous. Perhaps the first thing she would find, setting pen to paper, was that there was no common sentence ready for her use. All the great novelists like Thackeray and Dickens and Balzac have written a natural prose, swift but not slovenly, expressive but not precious, taking their own tint without ceasing to be common property. They have based it on the sentence that was current at the time. (That sentence) is a man's sentence . . . It was a sentence that was unsuited for a woman's use. Charlotte Brontë, with all her splendid gift for prose, stumbled and fell with that clumsy weapon in her hands. George Eliot committed atrocities with it that beggar description. Jane Austen looked at it and laughed at it and devised a perfectly natural, shapely sentence proper for her own use and never departed from it. Thus, with less genius for writing than Charlotte Brontë, she got infinitely more said.

—Virginia Woolf, 'A Room of One's Own'

Not so very many years ago educated and talented women were pleased to be told they wrote or thought like men, and often—in mixed company—they argued hotly that there was no such thing as a "female" mind or a "female" sensibility: there were only writers or nonwriters, thinkers or nonthinkers. Today, there are, I believe, few women who would be pleased to be told they write like men, and there is much thoughtful discussion on the question of the "female sensibility." What is it? *Where* is it? Does it, in fact, exist? What—if it exists—are its components? How does it operate? A tide of novels, poems, and plays written by women about women is sweeping over us. Many of us examine these books with a mixture of excitement and criticism born out of restless, only half-formed perceptions that not so long ago would have been rejected out of hand but today are the basis for a kind of thought and a kind of insight that seems to be in the very air we breathe. For these works, and our approach to them, are in many ways a parallel to the growth of the women's movement, which in turn embodies complex questions that, so far from being answered, are still being formed.

In a certain sense, there is a metaphorical shape to the growth of the women's movement that the novels and plays, both in their choice of subject matter and in the range of their accomplishments, reflect. For, if the movement represents anything larger than itself—and indeed it does—then it is the slow, difficult journey of a society out of close-minded defensiveness into the open contemplation of received ideas that no longer serve us well. The marvel of literature is that not only is it a detailed record of progress on that score, it is itself a metaphor for the digging-out process. Virginia Woolf's recital of the difficulties of Charlotte Brontë and George Eliot in relation to "a man's sentence" is an accurate parallel to the difficulties of contemporary women writers trying in their work to come to their own experience—even as all women, everywhere, struggle to come to theirs.

The subjection of women, in my view, lies most deeply in the ingrained conviction—shared by both men and women—that for women marriage is the pivotal experience. It is this conviction, primarily, that reduces and ultimately destroys in women the flow of psychic energy that is fed in men from birth by the anxious knowledge given them that one is alone in this world; that one is never taken care of; that life is a naked battle between fear and desire, and that fear is kept in abeyance only through the recurrent surge of desire which itself is renewed only when reinforced by the capacity to experience oneself: independently. The woman who knows *deeply* that she will marry and be "taken care of"—that this is the central event of her life—is in some vital sense handing over her experiencing self to her husband: it becomes a surplus weapon for him in his own struggle. She stands aside and looks on, grows drowsy and inert, loses the sharp edge of inspirited need, soon cannot remember—can no longer *feel*—the urge to act. Whatever nerve she has ever had, she now loses it and along with it the vital need to experience herself.

It is the re-creation in women of the experiencing self that is the business of contemporary feminism. Vast internal changes must occur in women in which old responses, old habits, old emotional convictions are examined under a new light: the light of consciousness. A new kind of journey into the interior must be taken, one in which the terms of inner conflict are redefined. It is a journey of unimaginable pain and loneliness, one in which the same inch of emotional ground must be taken over and over again, alone and without allies, but on the other side lies the freedom that comes with self-possession.

In this sense feminism is to psychoanalysis as analysis is to the making of art. Both the artist and the analysand create out of the materials of their own inner lives the magic of unexamined experience held up to a new light: a light under which new insights will emerge, new designs, new content. This new content is the art the feminist shares with the analysand and the artist. In the act of apprehending experience transformed, all three work hard to clarify a vision of wholeness that serves a hunger for internal coherence.

Thus it is with psychoanalysis. It is not the sudden insight or the moment of catharsis or the identification of trauma that is the analysis. Rather, it is the slow process of remembering, of recovering original experience, of holding it up repeatedly to the light of self-consciousness, that allows for the undoing of an old self and the making of a new one. It is the process *itself*—the damnably hard work of living with an idea long enough so that it gradually becomes the basis for a new existence even as the old one is disappearing—that is actually the analysis.

Art and psychoanalysis are both reflections of the natural process of human growth: the adult body rises from the childish form, the mature mind flows directly out of the early personality. All is of a piece, all clearly related, logically concluded. The conscious relatedness of one's entire existence is what produces the integrated self; the recognition that what one is now one has always been—to hold live in one's hand the sense of what one has always been—is to have oneself. For the integrated human being there is no past: there is only the continual transformation of original experience.

Culturally speaking, women have a past, and the femaleness of their experience lies buried in that past. To achieve wholeness they must become artists and analysands: they must break through to the center of their experience, and hold it up to the light of consciousness if their lives are to be transformed. They must struggle to "see" more clearly, to remember more accurately, to describe more fully who and what they have always been . . . If only one could describe fully what one is! Then one would be free.

Our culture is a collective record of that hunger to "describe fully" in the hope that consciousness will end spiritual bondage. We write, we paint, we compose to express as wholly as we can who we are: what our own personal lives have been. In the course of so doing we transcend ourselves, and the record of our lives becomes a record of our common life. What we discover in the struggle to understand our own particular selves is what it is to be human. The very elements of our own identities become a metaphor for the human condition. It is an interlocking process out of which we create cultural civilizations by confessing who we are, and in turn being told who we are. Inevitably, there comes a time when civilization must be told anew who we are.

For centuries the cultural record has been a record of male experience. It is the male sensibility that has apprehended and described our life. It is the maleness of experience that has been a metaphor for human existence. Literature, particularly, has been a vast reservoir in which has been cupped to overflowing the detailed description of human hungers and human fears as men have experienced them. The central image of a young man from the provinces going out into the world on a symbolic journey of self-discovery is the dominating image of our literature and it is, of necessity, a male image. In the twentieth century the nature of the journey has altered; the symbols have been reformed, the trip is now clearly an interior one rather than a literal one. No matter. It is still a journey that is characterized by a thrusting, piercing, aggressing motion: one in which man is pressing continually toward the center of his life, attempting to wrestle God, the elements, and his own demons to the ground as he goes. Naked, sweating, lost, terrified, he nevertheless pushes forward: defiance is the compelling force.

Now clearly this search, this voyage, this compulsive motion through a universe of darkness and pain, is one which speaks to the deepest impulses of all human beings. Thus, whether we are men or women, we recognize ourselves and make identification to one degree or another with what we find in the literature of our culture. Nevertheless, no woman could ever have written nine-tenths of the books that compose the body of our literature. What it took to write those books is a certain kind of arrogant self-confidence that has been utterly foreign to woman's life. This self-confidence reduces in men the universal anxiety of existence itself common to all human beings, and increases in them the arrogance necessary to aggress upon life. It shapes and controls the anxiety in a very particular way, pushing it back, creating a space filled with light and air around the human spirit in which the illusion of omnipotence is permitted to grow. It is a quality developed only by occupying a miniature universe in which one experiences oneself as a superior being. To a very large degree the superiority that men experience comes directly out of their relations to women. As Virginia Woolf remarked so dryly and so succinctly:

Women have served all these centuries as looking-glasses possessing the magic and delicious power of reflecting the figure of man at twice its natural size. Without that power probably the earth would still be swamp and jungle . . . [For how else] is he to go on giving judgments, civilizing natives, making laws, writing books, dressing up, and speechifying at banquets, unless he can see himself at breakfast and dinner at least twice the size he really is?

The irony, then, is that the maleness of experience which has indeed contributed so very much to the growth of human consciousness is dependent for its very life on the spiritual purgatory of women.

What, then, is the *femaleness* of experience? Where are the compositional elements of a female sensibility to be found? Under what conditions does that experience and that sensibility become a metaphor for human existence, thereby adding, as the maleness of experience has added, to the small sum of human self-awareness? These are questions we are only just beginning to ask, ideas we are only barely beginning to articulate.

It is my belief that the growth of a genuine female sensibility, like the growth of a genuinely experiencing woman, is a generational task and will be a long time in the making. Rarely in the work now being written by women does one feel the presence of writers genuinely penetrating their own experience, risking emotional humiliation and the facing down of secret fears, unbearable wisdoms. Rarely is femaleness actually at the center of the universe, and what it is to be a woman used effectively to reflect life metaphorically. What is more common is the painful sight of writers still in the fearful grip of female anger and female defensiveness: even as Charlotte Brontë and perhaps even George Eliot were.

There are works, however, it seems to me, in which one feels the heroic effort stirring: works in which the writer gropes magnificently for "her" sentence. One of the finest of these—chronologically not a contemporary—is Kate Chopin's *The Awakening*, published in 1899, and only recently "rediscovered." The story of this extraordinary novel is, briefly, as follows: Edna Pontellier, a twenty-eight-year-old American married to a Creole businessman and the mother of two children, is spending the summer at Grand Isle, an island off the coast of New Orleans where wealthy Creole families of the 1890s vacation. Between Edna and her husband—the rich, kindly, authoritarian Leonce—there exists an 'enormous gulf of spiritual and emotional sympathy of which he seems entirely unaware, and which she herself observes as though from across a great distance. But, then again, her entire life is observed as though at a great distance: blurred and without the sharpness of reality. Her marriage, her children, her memories of her family in Kentucky, her early fantasies all have the quality of dream and accident: nothing moves, nothing speaks, nothing makes real sense: at the center an awful stillness: a *female* stillness: an emotional inertness that passes for normal in the Anglo-American middle-class life of her time.

In this, her twenty-eighth year, Edna is roused from her interior silence. A friendship that has formed with young Robert Lebrun, the son of the family running the hotel at which the Pontelliers are staying, flames into open sensuality. Edna's desire for Robert—which remains unacknowledged and unconsummated—mingles brilliantly with the sensuality of all about her that for the first time in her life penetrates her skin, her flesh, her thought. She feels sun, wind, and sea as never before; always afraid of the water, she now learns to swim and experiences the sea in an act of narcotic daring; lying at midnight in a hammock she defies her husband's order that she come at once into the house, and realizes that for nearly the first time she is acting consciously, not automatically; from out of nowhere she finds herself saying to one of the Grand Isle wives, "I would give up the unessential; I would give my money, I would give my life for my children; but I wouldn't give myself. I can't make it more clear; it's only something which I am beginning to understand."

Abruptly, Robert Lebrun leaves for Mexico. The summer ends and the Pontelliers return to New Orleans. But Edna is a changed woman: bit by bit, the "awakening" she has undergone begins to dominate her life. She stops receiving guests, she ignores the house, forgets the children, spends hours painting, reading, thinking, walking, no longer hears her husband's voice. She is mesmerized by the growing discovery within herself of a separate, conscious spirit now making demands on her. When her husband goes off to New York on business, she moves out of his house and rents a tiny one of her own. Desire becomes an instrument of self-awareness: she responds to the advances of Arobin, a local Don Juan. Her hungers, now articulated, grow with inordinate speed. They become powerful, complex, demanding: and yet oddly sorrowful, tinged with a sense of foreboding. Robert Lebrun returns, and she forces a declaration of love out into the open between them. Lebrun, who is agonized by his desire for her, is nevertheless frightened by the extraordinary quality of Edna's new independence. He does not understand what she means when she tells him that now she belongs neither to her husband nor to him, but only to herself. As they are about to consummate their love, Edna is called away to attend the lying-in of a friend. When she returns to the house, Robert is gone. "Goodbye," he has scrawled on a scrap of paper. "Goodbye because I love you." She sits up all night, thinking. In the morning she takes the ferry to Grand Isle. She takes off all her clothes on the beach where only last summer she first came to life. She stands for a moment naked in the wind and sun—and then she walks into the ocean.

It is only in the very last paragraphs of the book that the force of Kate Chopin's sensibility reveals itself. As Edna walks across the beach toward the ocean, which she now associates with freedom and self-discovery, she recalls her thoughts of the previous night:

She had said over and over to herself: "Today it is Arobin; tomorrow it will be someone else." . . . Despondency had come upon her there in the wakeful night, and had never lifted. There was no one thing in the world that she desired. There was no human being whom she wanted near her except Robert; and she even realized that the day would come when he, too, and the thought of him would melt out of her existence, leaving her alone. The

children appeared before her like antagonists who had
overcome her, who had overpowered and sought to drag
her into the soul's slavery for the rest of her days. But she
knew a way to elude them.

What Edna has seen in the night is the elusiveness of life,
the power and insatiability of spiritual hunger, the meanness
and smallness that is our socialized lives. She has looked
into the future with a calm now drained of all conflict, and
she has seen the men replacing one another, and the hunger
of consciousness driving her on. For these men—Arobin
and Robert have helped arouse in her a wildness of longing
that far surpasses them, a longing they can never satisfy,
that nothing and no one can ever actually satisfy: for no
ordinary human and no civilized circumstance is equal to
the demands of that hunger once it is unleashed in a person
of spiritual dimension. Edna has put her mouth to the
primitive sense of spirit-freedom and spirit-fulfillment that
haunts the human soul, and now that she has tasted of
that exotic food, life without it would indeed be unendur-
able, a slavery of the soul. On the other hand, she cannot go
back, cannot pretend to the old ignorant life; she has lost
forever all hope of peace.

The swift visionary quality of Edna's insight—the sheer
explosiveness of it—is directly proportionate to all the years
of suppressed consciousness that have gone before it. If she
had been a man, pursuing life at a normal rate of developing consciousness, Edna undoubtedly would have arrived at
the age of sixty in possession of the same human despair:
"For *this*? Is *this* what it was all for?" But as she was a

woman—steeped in silence and unconsciousness nearly all her short life—the insight, when it came, came with pressure-cooker force: suicidal force. This perception is the power that irradiates *The Awakening.* This is experience transformed. This is femaleness used as a metaphor for life. This is the female sensibility in its most fully realized state.

In our time we have the novels of Paula Fox and the plays of Myrna Lamb as fine examples of the femaleness of life operating to illuminate human experience. Paula Fox creates out of Sophie in *Desperate Characters* and Annie in *The Western Coast* two protagonists whose significance lies in the womanness of their beings. Indeed, womanness is the compelling element in both novels. To deal with only one: *Desperate Characters* is a story of contemporary disintegration: a tale of human life sacrificed to the brutal disintegration of the city even as the souls of a man and a woman trapped in the equally brutal disintegration of an empty marriage are also being sacrificed. Jake and Sophie, a pair of well-to-do New Yorkers, live in comfort in a fine house in Brooklyn. Once an actively liberal lawyer, Jake is now financially settled and spiritually confused. Meaning has slowly ebbed from his work as well as from his marriage. Between him and Sophie there exists an uneasy truce. Their life together is marked by emotional silence, the death of passion, mutual suspicion. Inertia propels them forward. The city pushes in on them. Bit by bit, incident by incident, one feels Jake and Sophie surrounded by the filth, the menace, the hideous fear of civilization breaking down that is the dailiness of New York. Dread overtakes their lives: the city threatens and isolates them at every turn.

Seeking release, they drive out to their house in the country only to find the place horribly vandalized. In an anguish of helplessness Jake takes Sophie against her will. There is no escape for these two: neither without or within. For, clearly, the paranoia justifiably induced by the city is more than halfway met by the emotional desolation of their interior lives. A tension is created on which is balanced the two forms of deterioration. It is this tension that makes Jake and Sophie desperate characters.

What is most remarkable in *Desperate Characters* is the way in which the femaleness of Sophie's intelligence is made to operate. It is, essentially, Sophie's story that is being told: it is through her eyes, her thought, her experience that we see everything. Sophie is the ultimate woman: she sees all, understands all, records all, and does nothing. Her intelligence is trapped, inert, inoperative. She observes with the dignified paralysis of a categoric spectator. The choices of her life have rendered her incapable of action; she can only be acted upon. She experiences her life as though at the center of a void with the antennae of her observations surfacing only for a quick look around. Every now and then, desire struggles toward motion, but soon enough it dies down, overcome by the vast disconnectedness of her being. Life is a series of single shots for Sophie; the camera of her soul can register only the separate image.

The sense we have in contemporary life of being trapped in our cities, trapped in our technology, trapped in emotional death, unable to make the separate parts of ourselves cohere becomes very powerful when seen against the trapped inertness of Sophie's intelligence. For what Sophie communicates is a sense of inescapable destiny: the natural fulfillment of the abdicating self that is femaleness incarnate. And what Paula Fox communicates is that the femaleness is the best possible representation of the spiritual abdication that is modern life.

The plays of Myrna Lamb come directly out of the American feminist consciousness. Written in a stripped, metaphorical, surreal language, the plays, properly speaking, have a single subject: the corrosive antagonism at the heart of all sexual relations between men and women. Lamb's plays—nearly all of which have been produced in New York—appear in a collection called *The Mod Donna and Scyklon Z*. The best of these are *But What Have You Done for Me Lately?* and *The Mod Donna*. The first—a remarkable piece of agitprop theater—is about a man who awakens to find himself in a silent, empty space. Something is wrong, terribly wrong; he can't quite tell what. A woman enters, dressed in doctor's white. She speaks, he speaks. Slowly, the man makes an incredible discovery: he has been impregnated. The woman is in a position to grant him an abortion. The man pleads desperately with her to do so. The woman becomes his interrogator. The empty space becomes a laboratory-courtroom. What follows is trial and indictment. (The effect of the reversed positions is extraordinary, similar to that of a white man turning black or a psychiatrist being confined in a mental hospital. He says, "I don't believe it. I can't believe this nightmare." She says, "Well, that is how many people feel upon learning these things." He says, "Do you know that I want to kill you? That is all I feel. The desire to kill you." She says, "A common reaction. The impregnated often feel the desire to visit violence upon the impregnator.") Gradually, it is revealed that the woman and the man were youthful lovers, that he impregnated and abandoned her, that he went on to become an important public figure (who is actively opposed to legal abortion), that she nearly died in childbirth, never let another man touch her again, and has clawed her way up, bitter and traumatized, to this moment. The speeches she delivers glitter with hatred and survival. The speeches he delivers cringe with fear and the consequence of emotional ignorance. The entire play is a spectacular exercise in the art of sexual vengeance, comparable to Dürrenmatt's *The Visit*.

The Mod Donna circles closer, approaching the genuine target of Lamb's central insight: the obsession with sexual desirability that characterizes women's lives—its meaning and its consequence. Two couples—Donna and Charlie, Jeff and Chris—play a weird game of sexual musical chairs. Chris, driven by dissatisfaction with her waning desirability, makes Jeff take Donna into their marriage. Donna, driven equally by the dissatisfaction of her "unused" desirability, consents to join the *ménage à trois*.

The three live together, Donna and Jeff sleeping together, Chris watching and commenting. Donna's husband, Charlie, who works for Jeff and is humiliated by him, hates, loves, and is bewildered by Donna. He waits for her to come back, not knowing what else to do. Ultimately, Chris and Jeff betray Donna, going off to Europe by themselves, leaving her pregnant with the baby the "three" of them have begotten. In a final paroxysm of rage, jealousy, and frustration, Donna provokes Charlie into murdering her. The entire action of the play is a result of the maneuverings of the two women. As their speeches mount from self-deception to irony to rage, the obsessive psychic question that holds each of them in bondage—*Mirror, mirror, on the wall, who is the fairest of them all?*—stands surrounded by a fury of self-hatred: a fury that this, after all, only *this*, should be the question of her life, and thus the source of her inescapable destiny; for the questions one asks determine the destiny one receives. Each, then, moving with mad logic in an indisputably mad set of circumstances, thinks to cheat destiny at its own game, imagining that sexual manipulation will end sexual definition. The transparently murderous irony is, of course, the point of the play.

Myrna Lamb's work is, in three important respects, comparable to the work of Norman Mailer, and the comparison is here worth making. First of all, the power of her work—as with Mailer's—resides in neither her characterizations nor her dramatic plots, but rather in the force of her language. It is there, in the language, that the sensibility exists. It is there, in the shape and rhythm of the words and the sentences, that the story is being told. As the work moves closer to the bone, the language dives deeper and deeper, mounts higher and higher. We are caught in its anguish, impelled by its insistence, instructed finally by its pitch. What is actually happening to the characters is revealed to us by what is happening to the language.

Second, Lamb's language—again, as with Mailer—has a runaway quality to it: she does not always have her hands on the controls. Sometimes the language soars, sometimes it bucks and swerves, sometimes it sinks like a stone. But whatever it's doing, whether it's hitting the target or ricocheting off the walls—Lamb, like Mailer, is right in there with it, lurching, lunging, flying along, writer and language tied together, chasing down experience, bulling somehow toward the secret center of things.

Third, it is this compulsion to chase down experience, to penetrate the center, that powers the work of both writers. Mailer is driven by his vision of things. Not only must he be true to what he sees, but he must keep going until what he sees is *true*. He is thus forced to take emotional risks, to act with an emotional boldness that, win or lose, is exultant in its honesty. At her best, Lamb exhibits this same capacity for emotional risk-taking, this same need to press forward until naked sight brings us to the only honesty possible.

The importance, of course, of thus comparing Norman Mailer and Myrna Lamb lies in the fact that Mailer's vision is entirely a product of the male sensibility, as is Lamb's of the female sensibility. What he digs and digs for, forever trying to root out, is the maleness of things. In the course of so doing he transforms his maleness, and it becomes an imaginative re-creation of the life we are living. Myrna Lamb, in reaching for her femaleness, is involved in the selfsame act of re-creation. What she is doing is precisely what Virginia Woolf said would have to be done if ever a first step was to be taken toward a generation of great women writers.

The novels of Joan Didion, Anne Roiphe, Lois Gould, and the Englishwoman Margaret Drabble seem to me works very much in the grip of the awful power of lingering defensiveness and conflict too dreadful to bear.

The most celebrated of these writers is Joan Didion, and the book that made her nationally famous is *Play It as It Lays*. Didion's great talent lies in her ability to evoke the stunning abstractness of southern California "dying in the golden light." Her images of people alone on freeways, beside mansion pools, in supermarkets at three in the morning, at despairing beach parties, on blistering streets with curlers in their hair and wedgies on their feet, are remarkable and compelling. And indeed, much of this sense of things pervades *Play It as It Lays*. The scene is movie people Los Angeles; the character is Maria Wyeth: model, actress, semi-estranged wife of a movie director, mother of a retarded child; the atmosphere is California drift. Maria drifts through the days of her life awash in a sea of empty friendships and corrupted emotions. Sex, drugs, abortion, and death roll themselves up on her tide, and then roll themselves back. Frightened of everything under the L.A. sun, suffering nameless dread and severe withdrawal, she feels safe only when she is driving the freeways. Nothing connects, nothing holds. People, scenes, events present themselves, one by one, before the camera's eye of Maria's attention; the camera strains to focus; misses; next, please. Disconnected is not the word for Maria. Chloroformed is more like it. People in the book keep asking Maria what she is thinking. "Nothing," she says. The people respond variously with cynicism, anger, awe. They think she's holding out on them. The reader, of course, knows better. The reader knows Maria speaks the truth, for that is what the book is all about: nothing, nothing, nothing. Maria knows what nobody else knows: that it is all nothing; that we go on "playing it" exactly as though we did not know it is all nothing.

The vision of nothingness haunts this century, and it is not uncommon that that vision finds expression through the portrayal of a woman breaking down in the face of the void. Nearly always, the breakdown is one of silence and withdrawal accompanied by irrational behavior that is never illuminated, never explained. Inevitably, this silence is imagined as having at its source some spiritual mystery, a deeper power, a secret heart of knowledge. Very quickly we are in the presence of a primitive myth: the belief in the magical properties of "strange" (that is, unreal) beings such as madmen, saints, idiots—and women. The important thing about this myth is that it is created and used almost solely by men in the ascendancy who are very far from mad and very far from silent. Knowing less than nothing about the silence or madness of women, they have used this conceit as a foil for their own often grandiose notions of existential angst, and its usage has degenerated into hack formulas for those who have a vested interest in the most cliché ideas of grief and madness in the modern world.

In our own time, the absolutely best place to find a superabundance of these significantly crazy ladies is in the movies, and in no movies more so than those of Michelangelo Antonioni. Put them all together and Antonioni's movies spell Monica Vitti: eyes rolling in her head, hand stuffed wildly in her mouth, mute as the tomb, tearing blindly at her Givenchy dress while any number of men implore, "What's *wrong?* Just tell me what's *wrong!*" and the existential *meaning of it all* suffocates the movie-goers in their seats.

Maria Wyeth could have been written by Antonioni for Monica Vitti, so much a creation of that same usurped vision of contemporary torment does she seem to be. Which is not to say that thousands of women are not actually living out Maria's life; it is only to say that neither Maria Wyeth nor Monica Vitti tells me what it is like to be inside their heads. Coming from these two it's only hear-say. I am unable, through Maria and Monica, to hear these women speaking in their own voices or to feel them moving at the center of their own experience. What I hear and feel are the sounds and movements of puppets whose strings are manipulated by the fantasies of men.

I could not escape the sensation, as I read *Play It as It Lays*, that Maria's language was not her own: that her telescoped responses and significant silences had been placed in her mouth and behind her eyes by a generation of literary references created by an experience that was not the primary experience of the author. Thus, the story of Maria's life fails to become a convincing portrait of emotional removal; on the contrary, the story *itself* becomes an act of emotional removal. One feels oneself in the presence of a writer who believed it good to be told she wrote like a man, and has—with the tools of talent and intelligence—knocked that belief into place: a shield between herself and her work.

Lois Gould's novels, which have been described as "bitchy," "tough," "honest," are an interesting variant product of the same kind of dishonesty that plagues *Play It as It Lays*: the dishonesty of defensiveness. Gould's novels do not actually tell stories; they fuse in my mind into one long monologue being spoken by an upper-middle-class New York Jewish woman who "knows the name of everything" and has a justifiable grudge against everyone. This poor little rich girl has met with coldness and malice everywhere, and has survived only through the use of irony. Her voice is brittle, hard-edged, vulnerable, and mean-spirited. She indulges in a stream of confessional detail about her (mainly sexual) life which is meant to be brutally honest. Very quickly, however, one perceives that the honesty is only a fashionable honesty: one whose limits have been set well in advance, and will in fact expose neither protagonist nor author to any unexpected emotions or insights. The honesty is a ploy: the more she reveals the more she conceals. Behind the toughness is a swamp of self-pity, an overpowering conviction of worthlessness. The writer-heroine is sealed defensively inside the toughness—and she'll be damned if we get in there, inside *that* fortress. From this kind of writing we can learn nothing: nothing about ourselves, or the world around us, or what it means to pass through life as a woman.

And then there is Anne Roiphe's *Up the Sandbox*. Written with grace and intelligence, this book has been hailed as a work that comes to realistic grips with the emotional-social bind of women's lives. It is nothing of the sort. What it is, though, is an important instance of the overwhelming *fear* with which a writer who also happens to be a woman begins to even sniff out the meaning of her own experience. The facing down of that fear is the point at which the female sensibility begins to grow, the point at which one *begins* to "come to grips" with one's subject. *Up the Sandbox* is a work in which fear is capitulated to rather than faced down; the lack of courage is fatal; it results in a dishonest book.

The story, very briefly, is as follows: Margaret is an intelligent, educated young mother and wife. Her husband is a graduate student at Columbia. They live a shabby-genteel life on New York's Upper West Side, waiting for the husband to finish his studies so life can improve. The husband, of course, is not really—certainly not solely—waiting. He is doing: it is his doing that declares a period of suspension for both of them. But Margaret: she is *waiting*. She spends her days shopping, cleaning, taking her child to the park. She tries to convince herself that the raising of this child is the equivalent of her husband's work; that it is, in fact, life itself; that, therefore, the sensation of waiting for her life to begin is an illusion. But it doesn't work: the energy inside her remains muffled, trapped, alive, and insistent. This imprisoned energy is the subject of the book, and it is what Anne Roiphe does with it that turns *Up the Sandbox* into a *Ladies' Home Journal* story. Instead of gathering force and bursting through to *whatever* is on the other side, the energy of her protagonist leaks out in safe little puddles, its pressure defused in a series of park-bench fantasies. The fantasy life, to be sure, is rich, funny, clever; but in the end cowardly and self-defeating, shabby in its emotional use of self-deception. The chapter headings clearly indicate whether this is a "fantasy" chapter or a "real" chapter. The final chapter is headed "fantasy," and in it Margaret discovers that she is pregnant again. In reality she is, of course, pregnant . . . The reader has been had. The book stands revealed as one in which neither author nor protagonist ever had any intention of moving into the eye of the conflict that continues to hover like an anxious shadow at the side of the head rather than directly face-front.

For a clearer view of the intelligent and talented avoidance of conflict there is the work of Margaret Drabble, a remarkably prolific Londoner whose novels are currently popular in this country. Very well written and generously sprinkled with insight, these books nevertheless remain, ultimately, women's magazine fiction. *The Garrick Year* and *The Millstone* are two examples of what I mean. In the former, a young woman named Emma is married to a young man named David. She is beautiful and genteel, he is Welsh and an actor. They both speak the bright, hip, suspicious language of sophisticated Londoners, and have in fact married each other in an effort to "chain themselves to wildness"; in other words, to keep alive their capacity for honest emotion. Inevitably, she has babies and their life revolves about his career. The story centers on a year in the provinces during which David flourishes on the stage and Emma declines in boredom, jealousy, and a growing fear about the peripheral quality of her own life. In a wonderfully perceptive passage Emma watches David on the stage and understands what acting means to him:

As I watched him I saw at last why we were here . . . why he had been willing to submit me to unlimited boredom . . . In the last scene of the play he had some lines that came closer to him than anything I had ever heard him say on the stage before . . . All he wanted from life was to be able to express, like this, to a mass of quiet people, what he felt himself to be. It was not merely pleasure that he had there on the stage: it was a sense of clarity, a feeling of being, by words and situations not of his own making, defined and confined, so that his power and his energy could meet together in one great explanatory moment. It was not enough for David that I should try to understand him or that his friends and employers should understand him, for we subjected him by the pressure of our needs and opinions to amorphous confusion: what he wanted was nothing less than total public clarity.

What is developing, of course, is Emma's realization that she needs the same thing. What *happens*, of course, is that after a lot of funny, English-ironic tumbling about, Emma has an abortive affair with the director and David is caught in humiliated confusion on a pile of packing boxes with the company sexpot. The supporting players disappear, David and Emma fall into each other's arms, she realizes she can never escape her marriage, he offers her a new life: a trip to the East Indies where he will make a film. The last passage is full of wisdom about snakes in the Garden of Eden, but the story could easily have appeared in *McCall's*.

It is, however, in *The Millstone* that the emotional cowardice which is the key to all these novels is to be found. Rosamund, a rising young academic, lives alone in London. She hangs out with writers and actors and is considered a swinger. Each of her boyfriends thinks she's making it with someone else. What no one knows is that she is a virgin. Determined to rid herself of her archaic condition, she sleeps one night with a man she barely knows, and becomes pregnant. She decides to have the baby: alone, unaided, without the knowledge of the father. The novel is the story of Rosamund's pregnancy and the first traumatic year of her baby's life. The writing is perceptive, detailed, and indeed a universe forms around Rosamund's clarifying emotions. But what is at the heart of it all is that Rosamund wants this baby because she feels only the baby can love her uncritically and, therefore, only with the baby can she risk revealing her own hungry need.

The need to love, the fear of risking that need, the dominating power that fear has over us—this, ultimately, is the crucial and determining element in all our behavioral constructions. The need is primary, the fear is infantile, the dominion is the crippling yoke from beneath which we must struggle our entire lives. We struggle, not against the need but against the fear, by attempting to own ourselves, and to bring to our lovers not our fears but our fulfillment. What has ever marked "women's fiction" is capitulation to the fear rather than a noble depiction of the struggle to conquer the fear. What makes of Colette a great writer is the courage and density with which she describes the struggle. What makes of Didion, Roiphe, and Drabble lesser writers is the meekness with which they elevate necessity to a virtue.

Ultimately, our art is a reflection of the progress of our desires chained to our fears. The meaning of a social movement is that it rises directly out of a gut need to defeat the ascendancy of fear. That need becomes an idea which takes hold slowly, and slowly forces emotional—hence cultural and political—change. The novels I have been describing are, as yet, for the most part dominated by fear. As the balance shifts for women, as they move closer and closer toward their own experience, impelled now by clarified need rather than darkest anxiety, so will the female sensibility grow, and the novels that will then be written out of that developing sensibility will, at one and the same time, become a reflection of and a guide to the feminist project: the release of the experiencing self.

Acknowledgments

All the essays in this collection, save for the introduction, have appeared in prior publications, though each has been revised and edited by the author for this volume.

"James Salter" originally appeared in *Bookforum* © Bookforum, Apr/May 2013, "The Lust Generation," by Vivian Gornick.

The following essays appeared in the *Boston Review* online, bostonreview.net, between 2008–2014: "Alfred Kazin" under the title "My Hungry Soul: Alfred Kazin's Raw Materials"; "Hannah Arendt" under the title "All That Is Given: Hannah Arendt on Being Jewish"; "Erich Fromm" under the title "The Cure for Loneliness: The Lives of Erich Fromm"; *"Justice: What's the Right Thing to Do"* under the title "Right by Others: On the Theory and Practice of Justice"; and *"The Americanization of Narcissism"* under the title "In Defense of Narcissism."

"The Second Sex at Fifty" appeared in *Dissent* in Fall 1999.